# Wild Mother Dancing

# Wild Mother Dancing

## Maternal Narrative in Canadian Literature

*Di Brandt*

University of Manitoba Press

Printed in Canada

Printed on recycled, acid-free paper ∞

The title, *Wild Mother Dancing*, is an extract from Daphne Marlatt, *How Hug a Stone* (Winnipeg: Turnstone Press, 1983), 79.

Designed by Norman Schmidt

Cover illustration: *Dancing Alone* reproduced with the kind permission of the artist, Leona Brown, M.S.A. (watercolour, 22 x 30 in.)

Photograph of the author on outside back cover by Irene Peters.

**Cataloguing in Publication Data**

Brandt, Diana

  Wild mother dancing

  Includes bibliographical references.
  ISBN 0-88755-632-9

1. Mothers in literature. 2. First person narrative. 3. Canadian fiction – Women authors – History and criticism. 4. Canadian fiction – 20th century – History and criticism. I. Title.

PS8191.M6B72 1993    C813'.5409'3520431    C93-098197-9
PR9192.6.M6B72 1993

The publication of this book has been assisted by a grant from the Canada Council.

*for my mother, Mary,
and her mother, Aganetha*

# Contents

# Acknowledgements

This book is a revised version of my Ph.D. dissertation, "'Wild Mother Dancing': Maternal Narrative in Contemporary Writing by Women in Canada and Quebec," University of Manitoba, 1992. I thank the members of the English Department for giving me the opportunity to explore this topic. Thank you, more specifically, to David Arnason, Heidi Harms and Joan Turner for invaluable editorial advice and encouragement. Thank you to Daphne Marlatt, Katherine Martens, Janice Williamson and Marianne Hirsch, whose interest and support helped keep me going. Magdalene Redekop, Nina Colwill and Judith Flynn gave useful criticism. Carol Dahlstrom and Allison Campbell expertly guided the manuscript into print. Muchemi Wambugu gave computer assistance. Thanks also to my colleagues at the University of Winnipeg, who believed in me and listened, and to my students, who helped me clarify many ideas. And most of all, thanks to my mother, Mary Janzen, who showed me how to live, imaginatively, and to my daughters, Lisa and Ali, who taught me how to be a mother, wild, and (sometimes) dancing.

*Wild Mother Dancing*

# Prologue in the First Person

In 1976, I gave birth to my first child, Lisa. I had just completed an M.A. in English literature at the University of Toronto, in Renaissance and Romantic literature, under the heady influence of Northrop Frye's "literary symbolism." It was like falling into a vacuum, narratively speaking. I realized suddenly, with a shock, that none of the texts I had read so carefully, none of the literary skills I had acquired so diligently as a student of literature, had anything remotely to do with the experience of becoming a mother. Frye's grand archetypal vision had given me a framework in which to make sense of the bewildering array of stories that make up the body we call literature, but it was useless for coming to terms with maternal experience. Someone asked Frye about gender in class once (it was a timid question in the 1970s), and Frye replied that gender was metaphorical in literature, that we are all female, for example, in relation to God, Biblically speaking, and all male in relation to the nature, as the heroes of history. This made perfect sense in class, looking at literature as a self-contained body of work, full of interlocking, shifting, sliding metaphors and symbols. It was incomprehensible in my house, where the reality of my maternal body and trans- formed subjectivity were insisting their unmetaphorical otherness unpolitely into my consciousness.

Where, in the rich canon of Western literature, were the mother stories? I asked myself. Where, indeed, were the mothers, symbolic or otherwise, whom I might have turned to in that moment of loneliness and desperation? Everywhere I looked, in literary theory or developmental psychology, the maternal was imaged as other, unhuman; either the mother was imaged as archetype, "earthly vessel," usually with a double meaning, dark and unpredictable as well as nurturing, or she was represented as the shadowy companion of a child with infinite needs, a caretaker without needs of her own, who was somehow expected to be limitless in her giving, without professional or social support. There were few narrative models to look to, other than the Virgin Mary and her few cheerful imitators who survived childbearing in English literature before 1900.[1] It was a vacuum that drove me to re-establish connection with my own mother and her unofficial oral tradition, the collection of Mennonite "old wives' tales" that had sustained the women in my culture, in the difficult, heroic experience of childbirth, a tradition of secret, whispered women's stories passed on from mothers to daughters through the centur- ies. There was a huge gap, however, between this tradition, with its circuitous labyrinths around the question of the repressed maternal subject, spoken in the completely experiential language of my mothertongue, Plautdietsch, and the conceptual frame- work I had acquired through university education, a gap that I could not bridge. I also began to discover women's writing, a whole rich tradition of it, almost never mentioned at the university in the early '70s, and a growing body of exciting, consciousness-raising feminist theory.

Less than a decade later, with two growing daughters and a much greater sense of my identity as a woman and also a mother, sustained in part by a community of other women, I was back in graduate school, studying among other things the Victorian novel. Suddenly, I was reading dozens of novels with the "family" as a major preoccupation, and children galore. But – where were the women, in particular, where were the mothers? How come they always died in the opening chapter? Most of these novels had young heroines in them who got married at the very end. They often had aunts or stepmothers or elderly nurse figures around them, but very rarely mothers. What would happen, I asked myself, if the story kept on going after that? If the heroine gave birth to children and became a mother? Would the story be about that or would she die or otherwise disappear from the text, or be sent off to the margins as her mother had been? At the same time I was experiencing how difficult it was to perform two demanding professions, motherhood and full-time graduate studies, with minimal financial support for either, and a constant tug for attention between them. I became aware of how terribly absent, or at least invisible, mothers have been in the Western tradition, in narrative and social institutions, in spite of their essential and challenging role in the continuance of society, through childbearing and childrearing.

I began to ask everyone I encountered, Why do mothers always die in Victorian novels? Why is the mother always absent in Western narratives, even when the story centres around children and families? These are some of the answers I was given in the academy: because the mother did often die in childbirth in the nineteenth century; because novels are about transformation, and adolescence is much more interesting that way, in terms of plot, than motherhood; because the maternal, à la Neumann, Freud, Lacan, Jung, is unspeakable, unrepresentable, unconscious, associated with death, double-handed; because in order to tell the mother story, in order to make a place for it, you must effectively challenge the master narrative of Western history, which is to say, there isn't room for the mother as subject in the Western conception of narrative as it now stands.

I knew, from my own experience of being a mother, and from discussing these same questions with other women who were mothers (mostly outside the academy), that these answers were not enough. If mothers did die in such huge numbers during childbirth in the nineteenth century, why weren't the novels about that? Dangerous, heroic events, such as wars, in which large numbers of men risked and lost their lives, were written about extensively in fiction, why not childbirth? Having experienced both states, I could not concur that adolescence was more interesting or challenging than motherhood. In fact, I couldn't think of a single experience (except perhaps being born) that involved as much, amazing, transformation as becoming a mother. I also couldn't accept the metaphorical association of the mother with unconsciousness or death; this was not an archetype that made the least bit of sense from the point of view of maternal subjectivity. The "womb," in my experience, had absolutely nothing to do with "tomb"; being a mother required so much intentional, active consciousness every minute of the day and night that the old metaphors no longer seemed valid. In fact, they began to appear malicious. As for the place of maternal subjectivity in Western narrative, I could readily see that there wasn't one, or, rather, that the place of the maternal was an impossible, contradictory one. And yet, there I was, and there they were, all the other mothers, women with children that I knew, and whether or not we organized a revolution, our very survival past the ordeal of childbirth, our very being alive and wanting to speak about it, not only to each other but publicly, challenged the old framework to its roots.

Meanwhile, I began to write poetry, circling around the question of the absent mother, exploring the mother's problematic absence/presence in language intuitively, rhythmically, through sound and image. Through the writing of three consecutive volumes, *questions i asked my mother* (1987), *Agnes in the sky* (1990), and *mother, not mother* (1992), I began to formulate the argument of this book, supported by current feminist theory, notably that of Adrienne Rich, Mary Daly, Julia Kristeva, Luce Irigaray and Marianne Hirsch, that the mother has been so largely absent in Western narrative, not because she is unnarratable, but because her subjectivity has been violently, and repeatedly, suppressed. Writing the mother story, or mother stories, therefore involves confronting this "murder of the mother," as Irigaray calls it, in Western social history and literature, as a political act. It also means re-inventing our reading strategies, most of which are after all invested in the tradition that denied the mother subjectivity. While deconstructive and reader-response theories offer many tools for re-reading the tradition against the grain, so to speak, and therefore begin to make room for the construction of new subjectivities in language, it is really in contemporary feminist theory and fiction-writing, most of it published in the last decade, that the maternal subject has begun to be articulated in a way that's useful for rewriting and identifying the place of the mother in narrative. It is also in contemporary feminist writing, perhaps because of its largely antithetical investment in Western thought, that the possibility of cross-cultural dialogue has flowered, especially around the question of the maternal: a point that is crucial to my study of maternal subjectivity and maternal narrative in contemporary Canadian women's writing.

For the purposes of this study, I have chosen to identify the "mother" as a woman who gives birth to a child and then spends a significant portion of her time and energy taking care of it, that is to say, the biological mother who is also the active, caretaking mother of the child. I understand that there might be other definitions of "mother." For example, adoptive mothers would fit the second half of my definition, but not the first; surrogate mothers, as they are commonly called, though I think it's a misnaming, would fit the first category but not the second. Margaret Atwood's handmaids in *The Handmaid's Tale* fit into this category. I chose to limit my study to biological, caretaking mothers for several reasons: (1) This is the most common version of maternal experience in Canada, in our time at least, and therefore most typical and representative as a basis for discussing the contours of contemporary maternal narrative. (2) There have always been plenty of nursemaids and stepmothers and foster mothers in Western literature. In that sense, adoptive mothers have not been forbidden figures in the way that biological mothers are. Someone, after all, had to do the mothering, even if the birth mother herself had to be killed or silenced or sent off out of the story in some way.[2] (3) I wanted to look at the moment of childbirth as a crucial moment in the reproductive process and in the mother story. It's one of the most significant moments in the life of every human being who has ever been born. It's one of the most amazing and magical moments in human experience, and it belongs, in the case of adults, exclusively to women who become mothers. This is the moment that has been most envied and imitated and abused by men in Western culture, and sometimes also by women who haven't experienced it. (While I think we can make a case for "womb envy," or "vagina envy," I don't think the same can be said for "diaper envy" or "washing the dishes and the floor without pay envy"! ) (4) One of the many ways the mother's absence has been covered over and hidden in the Western literary tradition is by the proliferation of maternal metaphors that imitate the act of childbirth in some way, for example, "writing" as an act of labouring to give birth to a book, or making war as an act of renewing a country's vitality through bloodshed. Similarly, the mother's subjectivity has been made invisible by metaphorizing the maternal body, as vessel, as unconscious cave, prison, castle, tomb. My intention in looking at the mother story in Canadian women's writing was therefore to undercut the traditional metaphors of the maternal body and maternal activity, insofar as they re-enact the silencing and absenting of the mother as human subject with her own story. At the same time, I wanted to look at maternal metaphors that extend the mother's subjectivity in various directions in contemporary versions of maternal narrative.

There are of course other ways to talk about the "mother" and maternal narrative, and certainly many other ways to talk about women's, and more generally, human experience. Not all women are mothers, and even when they are, there's a part of them that is "not mother," that remains a separate and independent "I"; otherwise, clearly, the mother could not be the subject of her own story, she would have to be a slave to the reproductive process, a vessel, a baby machine, as many people have indeed wished her to be. While I do not wish to valorize maternal experience or maternal narrative at the expense of other subject positions, therefore, I do wish to argue for a politicized reading of maternal narrative that takes into account the mother's traditional absence

Wild 𝓟 Mother 𝓟 Dancing

and the reasons for it, a politicized reading act that is *on the side* of maternal subjectivity. I wish to celebrate in my study the presence of the maternal reproductive body in history, in narrative, and in language, and honour women's reproductive labour in childbirth and childrearing, without which, after all, none of us would be alive.

# The Absent Mother, An Introduction

When Athena, sprung full-grown and motherless from the head of Zeus, descends from Olympus to pronounce the fate of Orestes, who has murdered his mother Clytemnestra to avenge the death of Agamemnon his father, the goddess predictably upholds the right of father and son over that of mother and daughter. "No mother gave me birth," she declares forthrightly, "I honour the male, in all things but marriage. Yes, with all my heart I am my Father's child" (Aeschylus 1977, 264). Apollo, who appears out of nowhere as Zeus's emissary to help influence the all-male jury of assembled Athenians, seconds her vote with the following bit of biological wisdom:

The woman you call the mother of the child
is not the parent, just a nurse to the seed,
the new-sown seed that grows and swells inside her.
The man is the source of life – the one who mounts.
She, like a stranger for a stranger, keeps

the shoot alive unless god hurts the roots.
I give you proof that all I say is true.
The father can father forth without a mother.
Here she stands, our living witness. Look –
[he points to Athena.] (Aeschylus 1977, 260)

One might point here in turn to the tautological character of classical Greek male thought, symptomatic perhaps of its general misconception of the processes of reproduction and their relationship to social function. One might further theorize about the motives of a group of men in defining "justice" and "society" and "democracy" as the suppression of the mother's right to express herself in words and actions, and to defend her interests, including the safety of her children – notions that influence our conception of society even today.

Mary O'Brien, in *The Politics of Reproduction*, argues that men's fundamental alienation from the reproductive process, from the moment of ejaculation during copulation onwards, has influenced Western male thinkers to promote philosophical and institutional structures around the concept of alienation as a primary existential human reality (1981, ch. 1). For women, on the other hand, observes O'Brien, there is no experience of alienation in the reproductive process. There is neither anxiety of origin – unlike every anxious father, the mother does not have to worry for a moment about whether the child she bears is her own – nor is there a sense of distance between herself as conscious, intentional human identity, and as natural, instinctual reproductive body, since these two parts of herself are actively mediated through the unconscious/conscious, instinctual/intentional labour of childbearing. The moment of childbirth, O'Brien argues convincingly, is a crucial moment in the making of human history, since it is the moment when our continuity as a species, from one generation to the next, and as a successful partnership between nature and culture, is most clearly affirmed through the basic fact of women's reproductive experience. In Western society, says O'Brien, we acknowledge this moment as culturally productive by calling it "labour," and yet we negate its social importance by refusing to reward it as work and by rendering the mother passive, inert and often unconscious during the birth process, so that it appears that the (well-salaried) doctor is delivering the child – often with invasive medical procedures – rather than she. Throughout written history, O'Brien claims, Western institutions and cultural practices have worked to suppress maternal narrative and its attendant tradition, midwifery, which might have articulated women's effective protest against these alienating conventions. Throughout this same history, women have been oppressed materially and socially *vis à vis* their reproductive capacity, with varying degrees of violence.[3] "'Between the conception and the creation,'" remarks O'Brien somewhat wryly, "'falls the shadow.' Male-stream thought has not analysed its shadows, perhaps, with sufficient rigour" (1981, 30).

Western literature, following O'Brien, can be read as the repetition and re-enactment of the violent founding moment of Greek society, which the *Oresteia* celebrates as a vindication of matricide in the name of the son-and-Father. As Luce Irigaray explains in another context, "When Freud describes and theorizes, . . . in *Totem and Taboo*, the murder of the father as the foundation of the primitive horde, he forgets a more archaic murder, that of the woman-mother, necessitated by the establishment of a certain order in the city" (Irigaray 1981, 15: trans. and cited by Hirsch 1989, 28). Louky Bersianik agrees: "The story of Agamemnon is exemplary, and if society were not so patriarchal, it is this story and not that of Oedipus which would have seized Freud's imagination" (1988, 46). Looked at from the other side, we might read the Western literary tradition as an ongoing lament for the missing, silenced, absent mother and her mediating, nurturing presence, in social institutions and discourse, and in story. We might think of the Western artistic project from its inception, and including its alliance with Christianity, as an expression of guilt at this murder, and as a series of strategies to explain her absence, if not to bring her back. Julia Kristeva describes the social power of the image of the Virgin Mary in medieval Europe as a "mooring point for the humanization of the West, and in particular for the humanization of love" (1985, 141). In addition, during a time when women were being disenfranchised, it provided an image of female power, which appeared to be outside the father's law and thus offered comfort as a kind of "cunning double of the explicit phallic power" (Kristeva 1985, 141). On the other hand, as Kristeva points out and countless women could attest, the Virgin Mary, by virtue of her uniqueness and perfection, served materially to humiliate and oppress women, who were forever found wanting in her shadow. While the Victorian novel allowed women to explore a certain degree of narrative self-determination, in keeping with the individualistic expectations and new economic possibilities of industrialism, the conventions of the romance plot and the actual constraints placed upon women in Victorian society, as several feminist critics have observed, made it impossible for them to negotiate the distance between daughterhood and motherhood successfully. Rachel Blau DuPlessis points out a general contradiction in nineteenth-century fiction between the plot and its female characters, where "the female hero/heroine seems always to exceed the bounds that the plot delineates" (1985, 7). In order to imagine a heroine with enough freedom to circumscribe her own developmental course, Marianne Hirsch explains, the author is forced to depict her as motherless; male orphan figures are often similarly cast adrift, set free by their lack of parenting. However, while love and marriage in the case of male heroes by and large signifies successful re-entry into the social structures that will give them prestige and power (with their long history of displaced but still powerful fathers), for women the outcome signifies the death of her individuality: whether or not she survives the very real hazards of childbirth, her interests from the moment of marriage on are subsumed in the interests of her husband and/or children (DuPlessis 1985, 6-7; Rich 1979, 91; Hirsch 1989, 44-45). Further, her own lack of mothering, Hirsch explains, "rob[s] the heroine of important role models for her development, of the matriarchal power which could facilitate her own growth into womanhood" (Hirsch 1989, 44). As Sandra M. Gilbert and Susan Gubar point out in *The Madwoman in the Attic*, "What all these characters and their authors really fear they have forgotten is precisely that aspect of their lives which has been kept from them by patriarchal poetics: their matrilineal heritage of literary strength, their 'female power' which . . . is important to them because of (not in spite of) their mothers" (1979, 59).

Pauline Butling writes that "the Freudian meta-narrative which has dominated twentieth century thought is perhaps even more damaging to women for its direct attack on the mother [than the Christian ideal of passivity and serenity]. Not only is the mother rendered powerless in the patriarchal order by her lack of a penis, but she is also an object to be attacked, displaced, and overcome by the child in the process of ego formation" (Butling 1991, 13). Gail Scott, speculating on the difficulty of narrating the maternal at the end of the twentieth century, observes that "the mother's presence in language has been reduced to utilitarian function (the mother is not a person). Making it difficult for the little girl to break the symbiotic hold of the relationship enough to see the woman in the mother. So the mother always seems partly in the shadow. Maybe that's why she ends up . . . as a semi-Gothic character, a figure of *excess*, of *hope*, but also of terrible absence" (Scott 1989, 128). Contemporary woman writers, however, particularly in Canada, have begun writing mother stories in large numbers, despite these theoretical and social difficulties, and in defiance of the constraints of the Western narrative tradition with its long history of enforced maternal absence.

How do you tell a new (or old forbidden) story? How should we read these new (and remembered) mother stories, wrested as they are, not without anguish and sometimes rage, from the silent heart of Western discourse and its unruly, not quite colonized margins? What happens if you begin to read stories from the point of view of the mother instead of the child-and-father? Are we still condemned, as Peter Brooks insists we are, tautologically, "to the reading of erroneous plots, granted insight only insofar as we can gain disillusion from them . . . condemned to repetition, rereading, in the knowledge that what we discover will always be that there was nothing to be discovered"? (1980, 525). Or, can we begin to recognize, as Marianne Hirsch envisions at the end of her pioneering study, *The Mother/Daughter Plot*, a new, politicized model of narrative, not based on separation and maternal absence, triangulation and death, but rather on the intimate interactions of the mother with the world around her, and with her child? "Can we conceive of development," Hirsch asks, "as other than a process of separation from a neutral, either nurturing or hostile, but ultimately self-effacing 'holding' background? I would suggest," she continues, "that if we start our study of the subject with *mothers* rather than with *children*, a different conception of subjectivity might emerge. Although it might be difficult to define, we might try to envision a culturally variable, mutually affirming form of interconnection between one body and another, one person and another, existing as social, legal, and psychological subjects" (Hirsch 1989, 197).

Such a narrative context would allow also for the development of what Mary O'Brien calls for in *The Politics of Reproduction*: an intentional, politicized awareness of our gender differences in relation to childbirth, an act of recognition and acceptance by each gender of its respective role in the reproductive process, which she terms "reproductive consciousness." Such awareness, argues O'Brien, is crucial to solving the global crisis in over-population and over-industrialization, since it is men's unacknowl-edged alienation from the reproductive process and male anxiety over paternity that has occasioned their centuries-long subordina-tion of women and children and over nature in the first place. Reproductive consciousness, then, would mean responsible parenting (literally and figuratively) by both sexes, which could lead to a partnership in caretaking wholly unlike the history of domination and submission that has characterized gender rela-tions under patriarchy. Such a revolution in *reproductive con-sciousness*, envisions O'Brien, could bring about the maturation of subjectivity in Western narrative and in society at last (1989, ch. 6; see also O'Brien 1981).

The following chapters represent my attempt at reading contemporary Canadian women's fiction from the point of view of maternal narrative. Since mother stories by definition challenge some of the basic assumptions of Western thought, including major tenets of contemporary literary theory, these essays neces-sarily invoke an array of theoretical questions. I have resisted, for the most part, the temptation to get side-tracked into discussing these issues for their own sake, and address them only to the extent that they are relevant to the text at hand. It is not surprising, perhaps, that some of the most interesting examples of maternal narrative are being written by women who, in one way or another, have escaped colonization, and thus write on the very margins of Western discourse. It is these women's stories that interest me most in the present context, with their different sense of tradition and female identity. The women whose narratives I discuss here write from a sense of otherness to the Western tradition, either through lesbian experience, recent immigration to the West, the cultural memory of a radically different Indigenous heritage, or the experience of growing up in a separatist, religious, oral community. This sense of otherness exists in creative tension and dialogue with mainstream discourse in their writing and story-telling, a narrative space I find creative and exciting. I begin, then, with prairie writer Margaret Laurence, who was really the pioneer in fashioning a place for maternal narrative in Canada, out of "wilderness," as she might have said. I continue with Malaysian-born West Coast writer Daphne Marlatt, Aboriginal-Québecoise writer Jovette Marchessault, Asian-Canadian writers Joy Kogawa and Sky Lee (living in Toronto and Vancouver, respectively), and end with a look at new, unpublished transcriptions of oral Mennonite childbirth stories, recently collected by Winnipeg writer Katherine Martens.

# The Absent Mother's (Amazing) Comeback

Margaret Laurence's *The Stone Angel* and *The Diviners*

Margaret Laurence's *The Stone Angel* (1964) opens on the classic site of the mother's body in Western culture: the cemetery. Above her grave stands the "stone angel," bought, Hagar Shipley tells us, by her father "in pride to mark her bones and proclaim his dynasty, as he fancied, forever and a day." Laurence describes this angel as sightless, heartless and culturally inappropriate – imitation Renaissance Italian sculpture imported at great expense to wild Canadian prairie soil. "I was too young then to know her purpose," says Hagar, remembering her childhood, but she knows it now. " I think now she must have been carved in that distant sun by stone masons who were the cynical descendants of Bernini, gouging out her like by the score, gauging with admirable accuracy the needs of fledgling pharaohs in an uncouth land" (*The Stone Angel*, 3).

Most critics have skipped over this passage in their discussion of the stone angel's significance in the novel, preferring to focus on Hagar's character, her personal shortcomings, her stony heart, her spiritual blindness, the way she herself comes to resemble, in the absence of a "real, living mother," the stone angel in the graveyard, particularly in her dealings with men, her own brothers, father, husband, sons. But what if we were to take this statement seriously? What if we were to see the stone angel first and foremost as a patriarchal icon, "gouged" violently out of stone and carried across the sea to serve the dynastic purposes of an authoritarian, entrepreneurial, colonizing patriarch, who "didn't much mind" the death of his wife, as he tells Hagar, in exchange for this intelligent, headstrong daughter to educate, bully, and show off?

What exactly are the needs of fledgling pharaohs in an uncouth land, that can be met by imitation Bernini statues in cemeteries? How are we to read the stone angel as patriarchal text? Surely, we say, it is there to mark the mother's absence – but what a curious marker it is, that carries so very little reference to the dead mother herself, and seems rather to spell out triumph, a celebration of the father's social position in the community, than grieving for a lost love. To what extent is the patriarchal signifier, stone-hearted, blind, and giving the illusion of spiritual grandeur and permanence, *created out of*, and *dependent upon* maternal absence? This is one of the problematic questions that Laurence's text asks us to consider, at the outset. And more importantly, in narrative terms, where does that leave the daughter who is forced to negotiate the demands of a possessive, exacting father with her own unfulfilled, crying maternal need, and has only an imported, archaic, "gouged out" stone angel as image and role model?

Lynda E. Boose, in an article entitled "The Father's House and the Daughter in It," discusses the problematic kinship structures that govern the relationship of fathers and daughters in patriarchal culture:

In the anthropological narration of family, the father is the figure who controls the exogamous exchange of women. The woman most practically available to be exchanged is clearly not the mother, who sexually belongs to the father, nor the sister, who comes under the bestowal rights of her own father. The exchangeable figure is the daughter. [If it is true] that the origins of culture are synonymous with the evolution of kinships, then culture has essentially been built upon the relationship it has seemed least eager to discuss – that between father and daughter. (Boose 1989, 22)

Boose, drawing on Edmund Leach's theory of "complementary filiation," goes on to describe the peculiar "illegitimacy" of the daughter, who, unlike the son, essentially lacks parentage and is "destined to seek legitimation and name outside its boundaries. . . . When her patronymic identity as daughter is exchanged for one that marks her as wife, she is still the alien until she has once again changed her sign to 'mother of new members of the lineage' – which by implication means mother to a son" (1989, 22).

Boose's analysis goes far to explain the traditional narrative absence of the mother, in anthropological terms, since she is mainly useful to provide heirs and therefore expendable (and problematic) after childbirth. It also sheds light on the contradictory and impossible position occupied by the daughter in the patriarchal script, as sexual object "owned" by the father and at the same time forbidden to him – a contradiction acted out, Boose suggests, by the ritual of "father bestowal," whereby the daughter is "given away" to another male of the father's choice, so that the daughter's marriage is defined within a pattern of obedience to him, instead of symbolizing his abandonment and betrayal. There is an underlying, paternal anxiety running through this narrative script. The father's repressed sense of guilt over his desire to possess the daughter often erupts in "irrational" anger at his loss of her: anger that is very likely acted out as hostility *toward* her developing sexuality, a confusing message for daughters who have been previously favoured by their fathers, but a familiar one to daughters even today (Meisner 1990).

Second, Boose observes, there is a widespread paternal suspicion that the daughters, so valued as the vessels of familial sexual energy, may wish to follow their own, willful desire, instead of conforming to their fathers' wishes (1989, 55). The "objects" of exchange threaten at every moment to turn into their own subjects. This paternal anxiety is visited upon the daughters in the form of harsh and unexpected judgements: Boose cites the example of Eve, who commits the double crime of attempting to appropriate the Father's power for herself, and then – outrageously – sharing it with her lover. She is punished for this – extremely – by expulsion from the father's garden into permanent exile and the "selflessness" of motherhood. We might think of countless other narratives that replay this primal scene, from Cordelia and Lear to contemporary examples such as Catherine and Em in Sharon Pollock's recent play, *Doc* (1981). The speaker in Ecclesiastes gives rare and eloquent voice to the paternal dilemma over daughters in patriarchy, in a passage we might read subversively as a tribute to the exuberance and independent spirit of the daughters, and as a reminder of how consistently and completely this spirit has been broken down in wives and mothers and unmarried women:

Unknown to her, a daughter keeps her father awake,
　　the worry she gives him drives away his sleep:
　. . .

Your daughter is headstrong? Keep a sharp look-out
　　that she does not make you the laughing stock of your
　　enemies,
the talk of the town, the object of common gossip,
　　and put you to public shame.
(Ecc. 42:9-11: quoted in Boose, 70)

Part of the terrible expectation placed upon the "obedient" daughter, who is motherless by definition in the patriarchal script since she is given identity by her father, is that she will "mother" her father even though she is dependent on him, and lacks mothering herself. Naida D. Hyde has identified the phenomenon of daughters having to nurture and parent their mothers and/or fathers instead of the other way around as a form of "covert incest," often leading to deep depression in the daughters as they reach middle age (1986). Nancy Chodorow, similarly, links the inadequate relationship between daughters and mothers in Western culture to the oppression of motherhood as a social institution, so that daughters end up having to make up for the "lack" in their own mothers, to themselves, their siblings, lovers and especially fathers, an expectation that reinforces and reproduces the dynamic of oppression in the daughters' lives (1978). This is clearly the pattern of filial relations in *Oedipus at Colonus, King Lear, Emma, Little Dorrit*, and the second half of *To the Lighthouse*,[4] a pattern that Lily Briscoe heroically and somewhat quizzically resists toward the end of the latter. But as Mary O'Brien reminds us in *The Politics of Reproduction*, paternity itself is a slippery and tenuous concept, based on a principle of masculine historical continuity that barely masks men's alienation from the reproductive process, and that in spite of the solidity and longevity of patriarchal institutions is unable to compensate for aging men's mortality (1986, ch.1). What happens if the daughter's story continues past the moment of her "expulsion" from the family or sacrificial re-inscription within it, past the father's death? What if the story continues past the moment of her obedience and/or rebellion, past the moment of her sexual awakening into adulthood and/or maternity, past the imaginary limits imposed by patriarchy: what forbidden territory, what new uncharted wilderness does that take us to?

*The Stone Angel* confronts us radically with this open-ended narrative question. Hagar, the disinherited slave-woman, sent into exile for threatening the patriarchal script with her subjectivity, her illegitimate, unruly, female desire: a perfect model on which to construct a wild, new daughter's text, on into motherhood and beyond, though few critics have recognized it as such. Most have preferred to read the novel with its rich allusiveness to older texts as a confirmation of traditional, patriarchal narrative structures (Djwa 1972; Kertzer 1974; Swayze 1988). Jungian critics who interpret Hagar's story as a quest for feminine identity have been more willing to recognize Laurence's narrative challenge to the patriarchal script. According to this reading, Hagar is rescued from her identity of exile from the father's house through a process of psychological maturation, or "individuation," by which she comes to recognize herself in female-identified images of the Great Mother, instead of the male-identified patriarchal Father (Maeser 1980; Buss 1985; Williams 1988). In recuperating pre-patriarchal metaphors of the maternal as universal, psychological archetypes of female identity, for example, the Great Mother as Ground of Being, as Absolute (Maeser 1980, 151-52), the "womb-tomb identification" (Buss 1985, 14), and "death as the metaphorical equivalent of the Mother as well as Nature" (Williams 1988, 97), archetypal criticism risks repeating the absence of the mother as human, historically located, speaking subject. We are left the impression that maternal absence in Western narrative is primarily an individual, moral and psychological problem, as opposed to a socially inscribed, politically oppressed institution with specific, historically violent underpinnings. Further, the continued metaphorical association of the maternal function with death reiterates the patriarchal signification of the mother as stone angel, that is, as dead (absent) body and idealized (present) spirit. David Williams, for example, implies that Hagar recognizes herself as mother, "becomes" the mother, through anticipating and confronting her own mortality, which makes it possible to affirm her connection with her own dead mother, an identification she has understandably repressed most of her life (Williams 1988, 97).

On the other hand, both Williams and Buss recognize the revisionary nature of Laurence's narrative, *vis à vis* patriarchy. "Mothers," writes Williams, "are supposed to die. Or at least be exiled. And if they live? . . . Rewrite the story" (Williams 1988, 89). What we see in *The Stone Angel*, argues Helen Buss, is "a movement away from a patriarchal world-view that emphasizes cause-effect moral behavior based on logical rules and notions of rewards and punishment, towards a maternal world-view in which one responds to the needs of the present moment through a freeing of the positive values of emotion and instinct" (Buss 1985). Seen from the vantage point of a daughter exiting patriarchy, *The Stone Angel* becomes a revolutionary story of a woman who refuses weakness, selflessness and death in motherhood, to fashion her own self-identified story. The "wilderness" that Hagar flees to and in which she makes her home is neither the sinful, barren wasteland of moralistic Christian mythology nor a metaphor for the Jungian unconscious, but the uncharted new territory of the pioneer: full of exuberance and hardship, and negotiated as all new territories are, with difficulty, using intuition and invention and trial and error. Hagar's "problem," accordingly, is not an attitudinal but a structural one: how to live with dignity as a (motherless) daughter in/outside the patriarchal plot, and further, how to *survive* it, past the disinheritance and expulsion from the father's house and wishes: how to become a wife and mother and still stay alive. How, finally, to come to terms with the immense bitterness accumulated over a lifetime of unremitting social and material oppression.[5]

Hagar's much quoted "pride," generally understood as a moral flaw, becomes, rather, a sign of her moral strength, and a refuge – not indeed from "the taint of the dead mother" as Williams suggests (1988, 85), but from the deadliness of the patriarchal signifier toward daughters-who-become-mothers. The fact that Hagar can recognize the limitations of her pride in old age is, similarly, a sign of her moral courage, adaptability and insight. Constance Rooke has coined the term *"Vollendungsroman"* to identify a new narrative type, the novel of old age. Such novels generally involve what Robert N. Butler calls the "life review," in which the protagonist looks back over her life "in a climate of radical revision," under the pressure of impending death (quoted in Rooke 1988, 36). Typically, the life review leads to a recognition of past failures and losses and some attempt to ameliorate them in the present, through active grieving, and occasionally, through surrogate encounters that enable the aging person to say things that were left unsaid to loved ones who have since died. Hagar's confession to Murray Lees at Shadow Point is such an encounter. Not all aging persons are brave or strong enough to participate in an honest life review. Rooke reminds us how much strength and stubbornness Hagar demonstrates in this final act, not of repentance but of recognition and letting go, both of her pride and the fear that it protected (1988, 39). Her revision therefore does not recuperate the patriarchal script; her maternal gestures at the end of the novel do not imply her capitulation to the stone angel as signifier and destiny at last, but, rather, show continued defiance against maternal absence, and one more celebratory act in a life that insists on the possibility of maternal subjectivity and presence, right through old age and into the moment of death.

Think of how many of the binary categories of Western thought, which Hélène Cixous has equated with the "othering" and silencing of women (1981, 90), are undermined, brought together, and transformed here:

| | |
|---|---|
| nature | culture |
| instinct | reason |
| object | subject |
| body | mind, spirit |
| weakness | strength |
| rebellion | acceptance |
| wilderness | home |

Critics have spent much energy deciding on which side of the binary code Laurence's loyalties lie and interpreting the narrative accordingly, so that we have really a double set of readings of the novel now, one side insisting that "word and meaning" win out, the other that "nature and instinct" prevail. Hagar Shipley's maternal narrative moves past them brilliantly, dialogically, in what Kristeva calls "the graph of a motion through which our culture forsakes itself in order to go beyond itself" (1983, 89).

The Egyptian motif running through the novel also clearly illustrates Laurence's method of subverting traditional narrative structure around the question of female, and particularly maternal subjectivity. Laurence typically chooses names, images, events that sustain a multitude of echoes and meanings, including contradictory ones, to create what Kristeva calls "ambivalence" in writing: a disturbance of fixed meanings to open up new possibilities in language. Most obvious among the various Egyptian nuances that colour Hagar's story is the Biblical allusion to Hagar, favoured and then exiled Egyptian handmaid to Abraham, father of patriarchs in the Old Testament. As the disinherited, "illegitimate" daughter of the self-made pharaoh Jason Currie, and later as the abused wife of Bram Shipley, his alter ego, Hagar initially resembles her namesake. (Hagar, we might say, is attracted to Bram because of his "Dionysian" energy, which promises a kind of liberation from the stern, "Apollonian" outlook of her father; but, as the novel shows, Dionysian energy without female liberation leaves women not much better off than before, Jason and Bram being finally two sides of the same coin.) Unlike the Bible, Laurence's novel does *not*, as many readers have suggested, consign Hagar irrevocably to a lifetime of non-identity and marginalization, "mother of peripheral wanderers [and] outcasts like herself" (Maeser 1980, 154-55). This Hagar, unlike the Old Testament one, assumes centre stage. She insists on speaking, she takes us with her into exile, into the wilderness, where against great odds she makes her home, bears children and raises them, and comes to know herself, finally, as a self-fulfilled, joyful, furious woman. This motherless daughter may be sent away, disinherited, worked to the bone, but she does not die. Neither marriage nor motherhood can make her disappear. Not even the imminent prospect of natural death at age ninety can make this renegade

Christian say "Our Father." Until the very last breath of her body and the last word in the book, and through deep loss and hardship, Hagar Shipley, daughter-wife-mother-independent-wage-earner, holds her head up, proud even when broken, her own person to the end: "Bless me or not, Lord, just as You please, for I'll not beg" (*The Stone Angel*, 307).[6]

Another related Egyptian echo can be found in the reference to Meg Merrilies, the homeless, wandering gipsy of Keats's poem, which the ninety-year-old Hagar recalls during her attempted escape from a nursing home in an abandoned fish cannery at Shadow Point. These lines, Hagar muses, "give me courage, more than if I'd recited the Twenty-third Psalm, but why this should be so, I cannot tell" (*The Stone Angel*, 93). Joan Coldwell discusses the significance of Keats's ballad in the novel, citing a series of incidents in which Hagar chooses to follow "the gipsy side of her nature" rather than the stern Presbyterian side: playing in the cemetery among wildflowers as a child; marrying Bram, "the dark, laughing, carefree lover of horses"; feeling at home on the prairie landscape at the Shipley farm despite its social isolation; finding herself at peace finally in the woods at Shadow Point (1980). The feisty, adventurous, spirited young woman who insists on making her own, independent life on the ramshackle Shipley homestead rather than be "owned" by her well-to-do father, is well represented by the wild, Amazonian Meg Merrilies, gipsies standing for a kind of free-spirited valorized homelessness. Coldwell further suggests a narrative connection between Meg Merrilies, the homeless evicted Highlanders of Scotland, and North American Indians in Laurence's writing, a connection found also in Scott's *Guy Mannering* (1925).

The political link between Laurence's interest in the plight of disinherited peoples and maternal narrative is often overlooked by readers. Margaret Clarke's recent review of Laurence's memoir, *Dance on the Earth*, bears quoting in this regard:

Because of its simple diction we might miss the fact that [the memoir] is also an important theoretical discourse on women's writing. . . . Laurence writes a text which does not ask you to play with the body of the mother, to dismember it, through your skilled deconstructive acts with language; she writes a text which asks you to re-member the mother, to become the body of the mother, through taking on the ethics that Laurence pro- poses as the ethics of maternity. . . . It reaches out the hand of a dying woman, its language places that hand across yours, and it (hand/text) does not go away when the book is closed. (Clarke 1990, 72-73)

It is no wonder, given the rigidity of Hagar's Presbyterian upbringing and the ruthlessness of her disinheritance and exile, that Hagar should find comfort in Keats's ballad. But in linking the gipsy motif with such noted and privileged figures as Abraham (Bram) and King Lear (whose confrontation with himself and the universe on the heath is clearly being echoed in the Shadow Point scene), Laurence refuses to invest in the idea of women's otherness despite their marginalization; she insists on re-visioning the available narrative terms. In the world of *The Stone Angel*, Laurence shows us, the margin is the centre, the wilderness is home, and, perhaps most radically and surprisingly, the wanderer and the mother are the same. Against the archetypal, Freudian plot in which the mother's death signals the beginning of the story and her reappearance its end, and against the American version of it in which the protagonist must leave home and mother in order to have a life, Laurence posits a narrative centred *in the mother's body,* as memory and as text.[7] In Laurence's vision, unlike traditional Western culture's, the mother is not represented by the patriarchal signifier that proclaims her absence but by her own furious desire and her own speaking. And it makes her, as Marvin says, "a holy terror."

"I, the Egyptian": the fact that Hagar Shipley can identify herself as exiled slave-girl, wandering gipsy and pharaoh's daughter all at once attests of course to her (and Laurence's) imaginative agility. It also points to a deep knowledge of the contradictory nature of subjectivity in this text. "Subjectivity" is a questionable and much debated notion in contemporary critical theory. Paul Smith criticizes the deconstructed postmodernist self with its inability to act in the world, and posits instead the feminist "I," a subject that acknowledges its own contradictions and at the same time is an active political agent (1987, 151). Kristeva similarily envisions a dialogical "subject-in-process" as a radical, open-ended alternative to more fixed, traditional subject positions. Both definitions of subjectivity fit Laurence's vision of maternal subjectivity. The contradictory meanings of the Egyptian metaphor also underline the impossibility of the daughter's position in the patriarchal plot, as both illegitimate and "chosen": wandering indeed being the only way out of this *cul-de-sac*. And where does the wandering lead? To a recognition of herself finally as a being full of grief and the capacity to rejoice: the daughter giving birth to herself, giving birthright to herself, as a self-legitimized woman. "The greatest tragedy that can occur between mother and daughter," writes Marianne Hirsch, "is when they cease being able to speak and to listen to one another. But what if they inhabit the same body, what if they are the same person, speaking with two voices?" (1989, 199). This moment of recognition is where maternal narrative, constructed out of the disinherited, motherless, patriarchal daughter's plot, ends, and begins.

Wild ☿ Mother ☿ Dancing

But notice how closely this daughter-mother's text skirts the traditional paradigm after all: the Mommy coming to terms with her imminent death, recognizing herself also as mummy (*The Stone Angel*, 111). Nevertheless, in this text the narrative depends on the mother's presence rather than her absence; the narrative ends before she does. The prospect of her imminent death, furthermore, is not the tragic death of a young mother in childbirth but rather the natural death of old age. Like birthgiving, death has both a natural and cultural meaning; unlike death by violence or accident or ordeal, with its punitive and sacrificial overtones, "natural" death is an event that is universal and inevitable. There is no structure of privilege in it, no reference to gender or class. It is an event that can be anticipated and that must be finally accepted as a healthy, normal part of the aging process. The metaphorical association of death with the mother in Western culture has served to mask the universality and naturalness of death by old age, and has tended to reinforce the idea of sacrifice and punishment, "unnatural" death, as the cornerstone of human community. At the same time, it has served to hide the material effect of such Western male-dominated, violent social practices as war and medicine.

Adrienne Rich describes the dramatic increase of maternal death during childbirth in Europe during the seventeenth century, after the invention of obstetric practice by men, following several centuries of witch hunts, during which millions of women were put to death for natural healing practices, including midwifery (Daly 1978; Read 1990). Thereafter, until the end of the nineteenth century, death during childbirth became the norm for women. In the French province of Lombardy, writes Rich, not one woman survived childbirth in one year: "The specter of death, larger than ever before in the history of maternity, darkened the spirit in which any woman came to term. Anxiety, depression, the sense

*32*

of being a sacrificial victim, all familiar components of female experience, became more than ever the invisible attendants at pregnancy and labor" (1986, 152-53). Yet for centuries, writes Rich, "the disease was regarded as a mysterious epidemic, part of the curse of Eve" (1986, 152). It was only after a man contracted puerperal fever – the actual cause of the epidemic, which was being passed on as bacterial infection from one body to another by unwashed doctors' hands – that this tragedy came to be recognized as a disease that could be avoided. (The doctor, incidentally, who made the discovery, Ignaz Philipp Semmelweis, was professionally discredited by his colleagues, forced to leave his post, and eventually committed to an insane asylum. Twenty years later his claims were recognized and the disinfection of doctors' hands during childbirth became accepted practice [Rich 1986, 155]). On another front, as Nancy Huston points out, the metaphor of childbirth has been widely used in Western culture to naturalize and justify the practice of war: "How many times have we read that a nation which never makes war becomes 'sterile,' and that blood must be shed in order for it to recover its 'fertility'? How many revolutions have been compared to 'labor pains,' violent convulsions preceding the 'birth' of a new society?" (1985, 168).

By emphasizing the moral implications of Hagar's journey toward death, Laurence undermines the metaphor of the mother as a figure of death even as she evokes it. Hagar's recognition of herself as Mommy and mummy gets played out in elaborate formal terms in the fish-cannery scene at Shadow Point, where she simultaneously recognizes her mortality, her connectedness to other human beings, and her own inadequacies as a mother. The presence of scales here suggests a judgement ceremony, underlining the moral choice involved in this rite of passage.

Mothering is both natural and cultural, it is something that

Wild 👶 Mother 👶 Dancing

happens to you (sometimes by choice, sometimes not); it is also an intentional, chosen act, insofar as it involves successfully birthing and nurturing another human being. In Western culture, with its single maternal icon of the Virgin Mary, whose perfection is unattainable by ordinary women, maternal failure is inevitable. The Freudian developmental paradigm has tended to reinforce this idea by its exclusive emphasis on the needs of the child, as passive reactor to drives or environmental pressures. "The fantasy of the perfect mother," write Nancy Chodorow and Susan Contratto, "has led to the cultural oppression of women in the interest of a child whose needs are also fantasied, . . . creating a totalistic, extreme, yet fragmented view of mothering and the mother-child relation in which both mother and child are para-doxically victim yet omnipotent" (1982, 71). Chodorow and Contratto argue for alternative theories of child development and motherhood that "recognize collaboration and compromise as well as conflict," and that stress "relational capacities and experi-ences instead of insatiable, insistent drives [that cannot be met]" (1982, 71). Hagar's acknowledgement of maternal limitation, of failure, is therefore paradoxically the key to her acceptance of the maternal role – not, indeed, as self-sacrifice but as collaborative and conflictual interaction of adult and child, which is finally reciprocal, an experience of mutual love between mother and child. Hagar's bewilderment at recognizing Marvin's love, despite her failures toward him as mother, is an important part of this process of acceptance. Laurence's point in juxtaposing Hagar's recognition of herself as mother with the recognition of her own mortality, I would argue, is not to reinforce the metaphorical association of the mother with death in the sacrificial sense but to point out the similarity between birthgiving and natural death, as similar events in the life process, rites of passage that are inevitable but require our spiritual acceptance and understanding in order to be done well. Hagar's speaking the mother words "there, there" at the end of the novel suggests acceptance of death, through an act of self-nurturing that contrasts sharply with her previous gestures of unresolved grief and despair.

The mother becoming angel: For Laurence this does not mean learning saintliness, in the Christian-Victorian sense of selfless martyrdom, but rather learning how to live and die joyously, in spite of mistakes made; the integration of flesh and spirit. The dying mother, in Laurence's vision, does not disappear; death is not an ultimate ending, but another image of being born, into another element, the mummy transformed as Mommy as new-born child, gasping "unfamiliar air" (*The Stone Angel*, 307). "Can angels faint?" Hagar asks, anticipating her own amazement at such a transformation. The gipsy-rebel child-woman pioneer, the disinherited angry daughter-mother, courageously inventing her own story against the patriarchal script, insisting on self-hood even into the moment of death; the stone angel revisited as maternal icon, standing crookedly on the ground, with lipstick on, proclaiming female desire, not for a dynasty, but for her own children, her own story, her own feet on the earth, dancing: – this is the real, re-membered meaning of the deconstructed patriarchal signifier in Laurence's vision.

If *The Stone Angel* is a celebration of the possibility of maternal consciousness in a world that has been dominated by patriarchy, *The Diviners* (1974) is a warning about its limitations. The novel opens with Morag, writer and mother, "river watching," worrying about the future of the river and the environment, and the safety of her own daughter: "In bygone days, Morag had once believed that nothing could be worse than killing a person. Now she perceived river-slaying as something worse. No wonder the kids felt themselves to be children of the apocalypse" (*The Diviners*, 4). Her most immediate worry is Pique, her eighteen-year-old daughter, who has recently run away from home. In many ways, the novel is testimony to the "terrible vulnerability of parents" (*The Diviners*, 297) in the modern world, where patriarchy no longer offers even the illusion of grandeur and permanence, where women carry as great a burden of reproductive labour as ever but without the support of the traditional family system, so that children are growing up in many ways less parented than before; where the environment is gravely threatened by pollution and the imminence of nuclear war, and it has become hard, if not impossible, to envision a healthy future for them at all. As Morag muses, of Pique, *"My world in those days was a residual bad dream, with some goodness and some chance of climbing out. Hers is an accomplished nightmare, with nowhere to go, and the only peace is in the eye of the hurricane. My God. My God"* (*The Diviners*, 87: Laurence's italics).

Much of the novel concerns the problematic of mothering. None of the mothers portrayed have supportive husbands; few feel themselves to be adequate nurturers (Morag's college friend Ella Gerson's mother being the notable exception). Morag finds herself juggling the demands of career, child and personal life in a precarious, anxiety-ridden balancing act, which sounds all too familiar to contemporary women.[8] Abortion is a recurring topic. Morag's first novel, *Spear of Innocence*, involves an abortion; other people in the novel who undergo abortions include Fan Brady, Eva Winkler and the unidentified mother of the foetus found by Christie Logan, the Manawaka garbage collector. Each of these young women is portrayed as a victim, of the family, of male violence. Morag's own close brush with abortion involves her somewhat desperate, ill-advised one-night stand with the volatile and dangerous Chas, after which she vows: *"I'll never again have sex with a man whose child I couldn't bear to bear. . . .* It is not morality," she adds, "just practicality of spirit and flesh" (*The Diviners,* 270: Laurence's italics). The abortion motif underscores the vulnerability of women and the tragic implications of their reproductive capacity under difficult or abusive circumstances. Laurence suggests that "innocence," the traditional equivalent of "purity" in women, is in fact a recipe for tragedy and abuse. The novel demonstrates the need for intentionality and responsibility in the area of sexuality. Desire may be an innate and unavoidable drive; but acting on it humanly requires the development of "reproductive consciousness" in both women and men. Pique's anguished cry to her mother, "Why did you have me?" adds a disturbing echo to this theme, implying that the motive for reproduction (for both fathers and mothers) can no longer be taken for granted in the over-populated, over-industrialized modern world.

Sexual desire and maternal consciousness, while related, therefore exist in tension to one another in Laurence's novel. Mary O'Brien argues in *The Politics of Reproduction* that the separation of the moment of sexuality from the reproductive process in general has been an assumed (and perhaps unavoidable) right for men throughout Western history. For women, on the other hand, this separation is only beginning to take place, with the advent of birth control and the contemporary feminist movement.[9] This separation, which is being energetically fought by fundamentalists and other groups on the Right, observes O'Brien, is in fact inevitable, given the current population crisis, since women *can no longer* see themselves, or be seen, as merely reproductive vessels (1986, 191). Ironically, the absolute identification of sexuality in women with motherhood in the Western tradition has been accompanied by extreme (male) anxiety over this identification. According to Freud, the discovery of the mother's sexuality represents a traumatic moment in the child's development. The economic oppression of women, including their confinement in narrow domestic circumstances, is another expression of this anxiety. In fact, the identification has served to erase the subjective reality of both maternity and female sexuality, the Virgin Mother of Christianity serving as perfect icon to exhibit their absence in Western narrative. Laurence is thus engaged in a dual thrust: on the one hand insisting that sexuality and maternal consciousness are separable and distinguishable from one another; on the other hand, reminding us that sexuality and maternity are not merely instinctual moments of pleasure and gratification but acts with far-reaching consequences, and with a deep inherent connection to each other. Female subjectivity, as possibility and ethical responsibility, is therefore necessary to both.

Laurence deconstructs the icon of the Virgin Mary as a narrative tactic to explore this new imaginative terrain. When young Morag sees the face of Botticelli's "Venus Rising from the Waves" at a Junior League exhibit in Manawaka, she thinks: "This would be how an angel or the Mother of Christ would have looked if ever such had existed. . . . Like a queen in the old old poems, like Cuchulain's young queen, the woman beloved by all men" (*The Diviners*, 126), thus making no distinction between the sexual and the maternal as icons. Later, admitting her sexual jealousy of Pique and her young lover to seventy-four year-old Royland, Morag feels embarrassed, "wishing it were possible to teleport herself out of the situation, literally, in the flesh. The ascension of the far-from-virgin. Mars or heaven her destination" (*The Divin-*

*ers*, 237), this time acknowledging the contradiction between sexuality and the maternal in herself.

Another, related preoccupation in *The Diviners* is the indeterminacy of language and therefore the impossibility of arriving at any fixed truth. "How could you say?" the young Morag asks after seeing Botticelli's Venus. "How can there be words for that face, for what lies behind those eyes? There have to be words. Maybe there are not. This thought is obscurely frightening. Like knowing that God does not actually see the little sparrow fall" (*The Diviners*, 127). As the novel opens, the middle-aged Morag, overlooking the river, criticizes the words she's used to describe it: "Naturally, the river wasn't wrinkled or creased at all – wrong words, implying something unfluid like skin, something unenduring, prey to age" (*The Diviners*, 4). The differing versions of ancestral tales, Morag's stories of Piper Gunn told to her by Christie and Jules's stories of Rider Tonnerre from his father Lazarus, also serve to underline the subjectivity in storytelling, and the impossibility of arriving at a definitive version of cultural history. "What is a true story?" asks Morag in response. "Is there any such thing?" (*The Diviners*, 117).

It is important to note that this recognition of the undecidability of language, the unavoidable slippage in it – the preoccupation of every intellectual discipline at the moment – does not lead Laurence, as it does many other writers and thinkers of our time, to a position of scepticism or idealism. Hans Hauge discusses the metafictional aspect of *The Diviners*, the way it "puts into question the mimetic assumptions that lie behind her previous novels," together with Northrop Frye's assertion that Canadian writers of the last decade are describing a world that is "post-Canadian, [in which] sensibility is no longer dependent on a specific environment or even on sense experience" (Hauge 1988,

122). He concludes that *The Diviners* is accordingly "much less grounded than Laurence's other novels and stories [and] hence the impossibility of an 'environmentalist' reading" (Hauge 1988, 125). I would argue precisely the opposite: that Laurence's recognition of the unreliability of language and the relativity of human fictions in *The Diviners* is directly connected to the deep sense of environmental awareness, indeed anxiety, running through the novel. For Laurence, caring about the environment is another aspect of reproductive consciousness: one of the urgent questions running through the novel is, Can we provide a future for our children, and if not, why are we having them? The loss of belief in language as conveyor of the Absolute, in Laurence's vision, becomes an imperative to become *more grounded* in "sense experience," to locate ourselves as precisely and humbly as we can in place and story, as Morag and Pique are trying to do, to feel the earth specifically beneath our feet, so that we can become responsible earth-keepers, as we must in our threatened world.

You can see this process at work at every turn. Morag's preoccupation with words and the impossibility of finding the right ones to describe the river accurately lead her to contemplate not the abyss of language but the way human activity has put all rivers in jeopardy now: "Left to itself, the river would probably go on like this, flowing deep, for another million or so years. That would not be allowed to happen" (*The Diviners*, 4). Similarly, Morag's literary critique of Pique's melodramatic parting note ("If Gord phones, tell him I've drowned and gone floating down the river, crowned with algae and dead minnows, like Ophelia") as "slightly derivative," does not deflect from her recognition of the real warning in it. Despite her flat assertion, "Now please do not get all uptight, Ma. I can look after myself," Pique shares with most contemporary adolescents a deep despair about the state of the world and the possibility of a future, and Morag consequently shares with most mothers (and active fathers) a deep anxiety about their children's continued well-being. After leaving Brooke to make her own life in Vancouver as a writer and soon-to-be-mother, Morag, suddenly aware of the tremendous responsibility she has taken on, reflects: "She no longer feels certain of anything. There is no fixed centre. Except, of course, that there is a fixed centre, and furthermore it is rapidly expanding inside her own flesh" (*The Diviners*, 243). Indeterminacy, in other words, does not lead in Laurence's vision to the now-familiar post-modernist celebration of the arbitrariness of language as though it were an end in itself but, rather, amazingly, to maternal and (more generally) reproductive consciousness, materially, in the flesh.

Dawne McCance describes Kristeva's idea of the "dialogical subject-in-process" as a theoretical insistence on "'the *singularity* of each person, and, even more the *multiplicity* of every person's identifications, the "relativity" of his or her identity/meaning in language'" (1990, 35). Any person thus aware of "the fact that his or her order is divisive, and potentially violent," explains McCance, will in Kristeva's terms "emphasize 'the *responsibility* which all [people face,] of putting . . . fluidity into play against the threats of death which are unavoidable whenever an inside and an outside, a self and an other, one group and another, are constituted'" (Kristeva 1981: cited in McCance 1990, 35). It seems to me that this is the way in which Laurence's sense of the loss of a "fixed centre" operates in *The Diviners*, rather than leading her to a position of scepticism and silence.

Maternal consciousness, while thus representing an important and indeed imperative mode of perception, is not idealized by Laurence, nor is it a privileged position. The act of mothering is presented as a tremendously difficult one, filled with responsibility.

The discrepancy between people's momentary desire for children and the reality it entails is shocking. "Was it only for that reason, after all," Morag asks herself, "she had wanted to get pregnant, so her leaving of Brooke would be irrevocable? . . . How many people had she betrayed? Has she even betrayed the child itself? This thought paralyzes her" (*The Diviners*, 243). Laurence holds men equally responsible for their share of parenting, fathering, despite their frequent absence from the family, physically and spiritually, in this culture. Lazarus's haunting cry over his lost, dead children, "They're mine, them, there," reverberates through the novel; Pique's quest for self-identity is very much tied up with her need for fathering.

I say *fathering*, rather than *a father*, because it is important to distinguish between the kind of conscious, ongoing, and vulnerable parenting Laurence insists on in this novel and the reified parent positions we've inherited in the Western cultural tradition. (Of nine definitions for the noun "father," the *Oxford English Dictionary* lists one that denotes active parenting, and then it is accompanied by the requirement of "reverence and obedience" in the children. By contrast, three out of four definitions for "mother" refer to the activity of mothering [*OED*, 730, n. 4, 1,360]). It is significant that the fathers we do see in this novel are extremely vulnerable men: Lazarus Tonnerre, Jules, Gus Winkler, Christie Logan – against such "respectable" and powerful figures as Brooke Skelton, who can't bear to father children at all. In Prin and Christie Logan, Morag's adoptive parents, we see grotesque parodies of traditionally idealized adolescent figures – princess and hero, or as young Morag imagines them, "Big Fat Woman" and "Skinny Man" (*The Diviners*, 36). Despite their faults and their hideous helplessness (which perhaps has to do at least partly with their respective lack of parental models), they are presented as loving and beloved parents after all. "You were a good father to me," Morag tells Christie on his deathbed and means it, though she has spent half her lifetime running away from him. Laurence's point is perhaps that it's the *activity* of parenting that's important, quite apart from (and sometimes directly counter to) the problematic parent images we've inherited in Western culture.

After Prin's funeral in the Manawaka church where they've sung Prin's favourite hymn, "The Halls of Sion," Morag recognizes several things: one, that she too has been living under the illusion of the Cinderella myth: "Those halls of Sion. The Prince is ever in them. What had Morag expected, those years ago, marrying Brooke? Those selfsame halls?" (*The Diviners*, 207); and two, that she's frightened of herself: *"I do not know the sound of my own voice. Not yet, anyhow"* (*The Diviners*, 210: Laurence's italics). She has her own need, her own darkness, her own story to create, and can no longer afford to be chained to a distorted image of herself. Christie's response to Prin's death, on the other hand, is, "'If I'd had it up to me . . . I would have buried her my own self. . . . In the Nuisance Grounds'" (*The Diviners*, 208). This is his way of recognizing the tragedy of her life: Prin's adding up to little more than the "dead half-bald baby birds fallen from nests in the spring of the year" and the blank "sheet of white paper upon which nothing will ever now be written," which her head and face resemble as she lies dying (*The Diviners*, 204). But in the terms of Christie's world, it is also a statement of love and the possibility of redemption, the garbage dump being after all where he is most at home.

If there is to be a future for the Piques of this world, Laurence's novel clearly tells us, we will have to learn to practise reproductive consciousness, both individually and collectively, on a global scale. This means learning to value what we've been accustomed to hiding from ourselves and throwing away in modern industrialized societies: both garbage and parts of ourselves, unmentionable obsessions and behaviour, unsightly men and women, mothers, children, people of other races. Christie's vision, "by their goddamn fucking garbage shall ye christly well know them" (*The Diviners*, 204), provides a prophetic gloss on not only on Manawaka but the entire planet. Much of Pique's quest involves reconnecting with the landscape and stories of her native ancestors, whose traditions represent one alternative to the wastefulness of white culture. Where her quest ends, in this novel, is with the song, "The valley and the mountain hold my name" (*The Diviners,* 382), a renewed connection of landscape and language that stands, with *The Diviners*, as a protest and a lament against the contemporary practice of alienation between them.

# Re-membering with Mothertongue

Daphne Marlatt's Search for the Absent Mother in Language

The search for the absent mother is a preoccupation in Marlatt's writing, from at least *Zócalo* (1977) onward. The narrative implications of this quest are most apparent in *How Hug a Stone* (1983) and *Ana Historic: A Novel* (1988), texts in which maternal absence becomes a central focus, though each narrative also plays out images and motifs from her previous work. As Barbara Godard points out, all Marlatt's long poems function as loose quest narratives (1985, 489). Each employs the metaphor of journey to explore the interconnection between self, place and language; each problematizes these concepts through the relentless questioning of the processes of perception and the production of meaning. The idea of "quest" thus continually turns on itself in Marlatt's writing, in the opening up of new narrative ground, a kind of "spiralling," going back and forth, while moving into new space. The "spiral" or "spirale" has been identified by feminist theorists as an appropriate narrative model for contemporary feminist writing: in contrast to traditional linear and circular narrative structures with their inherent sense of closure, of completion and ending, the spiral offers the possibility of repetition without sameness, the celebration of difference along with return. In the words of Nicole Brossard, the spiral charts a journey from "women's invisibility to new perspectives: new configurations of woman-as-being-in-the-world of what's real, of reality, and of fiction" (1988, 199, 116-17: cited in Williamson 1991, 180).

Marlatt's repeated use of the journey motif to explore the problematic construction of self and place in language thus constitutes, in itself, a spiralling toward "new configurations" of subjectivity, in an ongoing "life" narrative that has become increasingly feminist in orientation. At the same time, the writing of female subjectivity, not as fixed entity, but as embodied, gendered being-in-process becomes more and more identified, in Marlatt's writing, with recuperating the lost narrative of the mother. Here is how she describes her writing project in a brief essay published in 1986:

In a writing that has to concentrate first on language, questioning the formulated, the already-said every step of the way, form comes second, not as an easy mold to fall into a current to drift along with, but a struggle that is one with the struggle to subvert the rational/lawful language of the Father as patriarch & reinstate or recreate the imaginary/sensory language of the Mother as matrix of being-in-relation. ("writing in order to be" 1986, 67)

Marlatt's emphasis on the maternal as a model for female subjectivity, and as an alternative to the name and law of the father as the operative function of language, revises not only male-centred models of subjectivity and representation, but also much of contemporary feminist theory. As Marianne Hirsch points out, the predominant metaphor for female relationships in the feminist movement, until recently, has been "sisterhood," a model whose effect is "to isolate feminist discourse within one generation and banish feminists who are mothers to the 'mother-closet'" (1989, 164). The model of sisterhood, unfortunately, argues Hirsch, encourages women to continue to see themselves as daughters, rather than mature women, a position that is reinforced by the pervasive metaphor of daughterhood in the academy (1989, 164-65). It is only very recently that feminist theorists have begun to affirm the maternal as a model for female subjectivity. In North America, this shift began probably with the appearance of Adrienne Rich's *Of Woman Born* (1976); in Europe, with the work of Hélène Cixous, Luce Irigaray and Julia Kristeva.

Hirsch identifies four areas of avoidance and discomfort with the maternal, which, she argues, account for the ongoing ambivalence toward the maternal in feminist thought: (1) "the perception that motherhood remains a patriarchal construction," that is to say, buying into the idea of the mother as a unified subject and ignoring her multiple and divided subjectivity within patriarchy; (2) discomfort with the "vulnerabilities and dependencies of maternity" which are tied up with the vulnerability/power of the maternal body; (3) fear of the body and, especially, the connection of maternity with sexuality; and (4) ongoing ambivalence toward power, authority and, particularly, anger in feminist discourse (1989, 165-66). Adrienne Rich calls these kinds of anxiety about the maternal in women "matrophobia," a dynamic she describes as "a womanly splitting of the self, in the desire to become purged once and for all of our mothers' bondage" (1986, 236). Many contemporary feminist critics echo a similar ambivalence toward the mother in their responses to female narratives. Mary Jacobus, for example, in a recent article on Virginia Woolf and Freud, despite her claim for "an alternative feminist reading" of *To the Lighthouse*, re-inscribes the Victorian idea that the mother must die in order for the daughter to have a story: "If Lily's line at the end of the novel is the emblem of minimal but fixed difference which secures her self-inscription, the price Lily pays for finishing her picture is the casting out of the mother, her beloved Mrs. Ramsay. Or Mrs. Ramsay dies suddenly so that the 'third stroke' may be appropriated not only for Lily's art, but for Woolf's writing" (1988, 109). An even more alarming view of the maternal as "archaic and all-encompassing," a monstrous, threatening space whose bondage must be confronted and escaped by the daughter, is evident in Claire Kahane's recent essay on Gothic fiction, "The Gothic Mirror" (1985). Kahane conflates the body of the absent mother in such narratives as *The Mysteries of Udolpho* and *Jane Eyre*[10] with the imprisoning space of the castle, in which the daughter-heroine is forced to undergo a series of tortures before escaping into the safety of marriage. Quoting Leslie Fiedler, Kahane describes the dungeon underneath the castle as maternal body, symbolically identifying womb with imprisoning tomb. In Fiedler's words, "Beneath the crumbling shell of paternal authority, lies the maternal blackness, imagined by the gothic writer as a prison, a torture chamber" (Fiedler 1966: quoted in Kahane 1985, 336).

Fiedler and Kahane's interpretation of Gothic space is upsetting for a variety of reasons. It ignores human agency in the perpetration of violence; both writers overlook the fact that it is the prison-keeper who inflicts torture upon his prisoners, not the space itself. It ignores the critical role of gender in the history of power relations; the fact that it is female heroines being tortured by male torturers is completely overlooked in this reading of Gothic convention. Further, by identifying the castle space as both maternal and deadly, Kahane's reading denies the mother's subjectivity and upholds her absence as a necessary feature in the heroine's development. This argument completely overlooks the daughter's need for maternal parenting, and ensures in advance that she too will disappear from the narrative at the point of maturity and motherhood. It also negates the life-giving, generative function of the human womb – which in reality has nothing whatsoever to do with death. An alternative reading, I propose, would show how the daughter's development is arrested by her mother's absence; how the mother's disappearance signals the daughter's entry into the unprotected world of male aggression, and that it is only in confronting her own terror and lack of mothering that the heroine is able to escape from male violence into the relative safety of romance. The castle space as image of "maternal blackness," in this reading, becomes an imaginative projection of the male aggressors, since it is surely their own fear of death, their humanness and vulnerability, that these men are attempting to suppress through their violent misogyny.

The story of mother and daughter – what Rich calls the "great unwritten story" of Western culture – once we begin to imagine it, listen for it, is first and foremost a tragic one. In denying women, and particularly mothers, social power, in silencing the older maternal voice, which would protest this loss of place and power, and privileging instead the voices of younger women who exist in a daughterly relation to patriarchy, Western culture has inscribed alienation in the mother-daughter relationship. There is very little acknowledged space in Western social narrative in which they might talk with one another, where daughters might learn from and struggle against their mothers, and mothers might nurture, protect and struggle with their daughters. There are few models of what Italian feminists at the Milan Women's Bookstore call "symbolic motherhood," a social contract legitimizing "women's full social agency and accountability to other women" (Knutson 1988, 7). Instead, there is a proliferation of stories about daughters who must escape the suffocating influence of their mothers, to enter a male-defined symbolic space that will eventually silence them as well.

Marlatt's interest in recuperating the maternal in language must be seen against this background of absence and violence toward the maternal feminine, in both social and literary practices. In many ways Marlatt's work is consonant with Margaret Laurence's: her haunting question, "how hug a stone," deliberately echoes Laurence's "stone angel" in the Manawaka cemetery. Ana Historic / Annie / Ana Richards / Annie Torrent, like Hagar Shipley and Morag Gunn, begins to fashion the mother story out of a daughter's sense of loss and outrage and mourning. In each case, this process leads to a sense of renewal in the text, and the replacement of mothering for the orphaned daughter in other relationships, particularly relationships with other women. This latter sense of community among women is much more prominent in Marlatt's work than in Laurence's, largely due to the influence of the feminist movement in recent decades. Marlatt's writing is also much more self-conscious about genre and the linguistic process than Laurence's; we can see here the influence of the Black Mountain poets, postmodernism and feminist theory on her work. There is an ongoing, continually evolving narrative in Marlatt's writing around the question of female subjectivity, particularly as it relates to the maternal. While in the earlier texts the mother figures mainly as absence, or fragmented, indefinite memory, as longing, she gradually becomes more explicit in

Marlatt's writing, as lost subject mourned by her orphaned daughter, and increasingly also, as speaker-narrator, and finally, as a characteristic feature of language itself.

*Zócalo* describes a journey by a woman narrator, accompanied by her male lover, to Mexico, to visit among other places the ancient Aztec ruins of Yucatán. The maternal enters the narrative enigmatically, circumspectly, as metaphor, and wishful idea, pointed to in dreams and bits of old legend. At the Pyramid of the Magician, for example, the narrator encounters the following story: "It begins with a dwarf whose mother was a witch & hatched him out of an egg (so far back in time it can't even be told with any probity). She sent him off to challenge the king & the king said build a palace overnight or I'll kill you. His mother helped of course with magic. . . . So the dwarf got to be king of Uxmal & she went off to live with a serpent in a waterhole"(*Zócalo*, 56). The legend stays with the narrator as she climbs the pyramid and walks through caves. Intrigued, she looks for traces of maternal magic in the ruins around her, in their shapes and names, but the only trace she finds is the "oval stone body of his giant, its contour surely female" (*Zócalo*, 58). Struck by the "disparity between act & legend, the slow historical process of this palace built stage by stage by men toiling in the light of day – & the legend of its creation overnight by a woman, out of a spell" (*Zócalo*, 58), the narrator continues her musing about maternal presence in the Mexican landscape despite lack of concrete evidence: "And continuing her descent, wonders, under the name? dry land, no water anywhere, but caves, caves. Somehow the witch persists, chaotic mother, though all the images are male" (*Zócalo*, 59). As Barbara Godard observes, the maternal remains "an elusive sign" in this text, "apprehended by the reader's senses rather than by logic 'under the name,' on the near side of language" (1985, 491).

"In the Month of Hungry Ghosts" (1979) is a long poem describing Marlatt's journey to Malaysia, the home of her childhood, accompanied by her father and sister after her mother's death. Here the absent mother assumes a more tangible, close-up presence as the dead woman grieved by her family. Seen in glimpses of childhood memory, bits of anecdotes, held in the landscape of the narrator's childhood, the mother begins to assume the shape of memory itself, *"mer-mer-os"* ("In the Month of Hungry Ghosts," 55). Trying to find connections with this lost mother, the narrator remembers a second mother figure, Amah, her childhood nurse, whom she had forgotten. Barbara Godard describes the effect of this doubled image in the text as follows:

Between these two mothers, mind and body split. The mem sahib "had the words, & the words could not command their lives, only their hands" (p. 82), and has gone into the "black river" of death: Amah had the body, nourished and played with the children in a separate kingdom, in a world of revolt against the word: "two mothers, two but one mother & the other someone we have claim to" (p. 80) (Godard 1985, 491).

Another effect of this doubling is a separation between the mother as titular head of the household and mother as caretaker, nurturer, a differentiation that can only happen in privileged households with servants, or, as several feminist theorists have argued, if parenting is shared between both parents, or by a community of caretakers (Ruddick 1980; Dinnerstein 1977). Lynda E. Boose's observation that the mother is expendable in the patriarchal family after she has given birth to an heir (1989) of course depends on a similar differentiation. In juxtaposing the images of "Amah," the nurse, with the mother, "Mem sahib," Marlatt further highlights the treacherous duplicity of the maternal role in a male-dominated colonial hierarchy; as head of the house, the wife has power over the servants and children, however, with neither access to the range of social options available to men, nor the consolation of direct, physical contact with the children, she is left deeply alienated, personally irrelevant, alone: "what the Mem says goes (sometimes). what the Mem says exists as a separate entity in the house, to be listened to & walked around, with suitable contrition if asked (giggling in the back rooms) but separate, separate from the way life moves on" ("In the Month of Hungry Ghosts," 80). The mother in this text is thus pictured as profoundly absent in the subjective sense, even though she carries a name linked with power. To the daughter, she appears to be predominantly a figure of loss and alienation, buried by the words surrounding and embalming her: mem sahib, mah mee, mummy, mah jong, *mata, mata hari* ("In the Month of Hungry Ghosts," 58).

"In the Month of Hungry Ghosts" ends with a moving lament to the mother, expressing the narrator's outrage at this tragic outcome:

"life's cheat," deprived of any truth, as you,
long in tooth & nameless, recede from imagination: one cloud
of thought, one word of no earthly use, "mother" –

you knew the
dark, conspiracy, how they keep power in their hands, unnamed (you forgot, we give ourselves up to). you taught me fear
but not how to fight. you, misspelled, gave yourself to the dark
of some other light, leaving me here with the words, with fear,
love, & a need to keep speaking ("In the Month of Hungry
Ghosts," 95)

The speaker's grief and "need to keep speaking" suggest the possibility of rewriting the story, of reinscribing the mother in the narrative, beyond and against her prescribed absence. This question takes us into Marlatt's subsequent texts and their attempts to create narrative space for the maternal, in a variety of ways. The new narrative is foreshadowed here, by the speaker's preliminary act of calling up a new "word . seed . season" out of the old order, which has been irrevocably broken by her anger ("In the Month of Hungry Ghosts," 83). The image of renewal is of "garden paths, seed beds, tiny trunks all split open at last," ending with the invocation, "there mother-daughter, i call you up through the spring . . . whole, it [word, seed, season] comes back, it fills always where you were" ("In the Month of Hungry Ghosts," 83).

There is a strong echo of the Demeter/Kore myth in this closing passage, with the added twist that here it is the orphaned daughter who calls the mother (who is also a daughter) back to life. Not a lot has been written about the peculiar situation of contemporary feminist women, whose increased sense of opportunity and professional accomplishment situates them in a maternal relationship to their own mothers. Naida D. Hyde suggests that mothers who demand mothering from their daughters violate their daughters' personal boundaries and set up a dynamic of "covert incest" between them: "For the daughter to become her mother's caretaker," writes Hyde, "is clearly role reversal and parentification of the child. It is a betrayal by the mother of the child's trust in her mother to love her and take care of her" (1986, 79). The effect on the daughter, explains Hyde, is that she is "unable [thereafter] to protect herself from others' neediness and invasion of her" (1986, 80). Hyde's solution is to promote recognition and therapeutic revision of this dynamic in families. She does not address the fact, however, that in the wake of contemporary feminism, which has had its main effect on younger women, almost all daughters find themselves in a position of power *vis à vis* their own mothers. This was so also before the current wave of feminism, since in the patriarchal family the daughter was privileged at the mother's expense. In this regard, society has not got very far in revising the social script for women, and won't, until it succeeds in addressing the oppression of motherhood, as both institution and experience.

What is a daughter to do in this situation? "One might, in this instance," writes Gail Scott, "displace the memory category of mothers (so often negative, restricted, unaccomplished professionally) to . . . literary mothers" (1989, 20). Or, Scott suggests, we might proceed by remembering, "discovering the images behind the images, until we hear the tinkling laughter of Queen Titania (dim reflection of a murdered goddess) – who prefers an ass to her king" (1989, 20). In this sense, every feminist daughter must accept, in her adulthood, the task of calling back, remembering, and taking care of her absent, silenced, dispossessed, lost mother(s). She cannot do so unless she receives nurturing, mothering, herself somewhere. Otherwise she merely repeats the old pattern. In Marlatt's version, the cycle begins to be broken with the daughter's grief and anger at her mother's absence; thereafter, her texts engage increasingly with the task of recreating the mother as subject of her own story, as presence.[11]

*What Matters*, a collection of poems and journal entries written from 1968 to 1970, was published in 1980. It therefore exists in the uneasy position of both before and after "In the Month of Hungry Ghosts," in a chronological account of Marlatt's preoccupation with the mother story. Narratively speaking, *What Matters* documents the author's experience of giving birth to a son, Kit, and her entry into the subjectivity of motherhood, a rite of passage that coincides in Marlatt's case with the disruption of the traditional romance/marriage plot and moving into independent, self-defined female identity. Theoretically, the text explores the possibilities and effects of language, a commentary on the writing process while in the midst of it. Passages such as the following abound:

the writing is basically trying to tell the way it is –
part recording what's there & part voicing a state of mind
(each does dwell inside his/her head, sees out from there)
essentially circular
                but feel need in "telling a story" to
work towards some "climax", which means imposing a "plot-line" no matter how minimal?
                the "plot-line" is the drift, which circles back on itself while still moving towards some recognition – this rather than a plotted crescendo of conflict & resolution. (*What Matters*, 71)

At the same time, Marlatt expresses a growing need to create a semantic/narrative space in which to voice the newly found experience of mothering. One of the first references to the mother associates her with darkness: "Kelly said I'm drawn to those men who deal with 'the outer processes of intellect' & fear the 'vulvary darks of the mind.' this probably so – a fear I share with Al? of the mother, of being suffocated in the dark?" (*What Matters*, 72).

This passage is followed almost immediately by an image of the birth process, in which the maternal is identified again as "the dark & the unknown, that which we are born out of." Most striking here is Marlatt's minute attention to the birthing itself, without any mention whatsoever of the mother as human subject, actively and consciously mediating the birth with her labour. The "mother" is imagined as wholly body, unconscious, threatening, chaotic, though at the same time intentional, fecund:

infant at mercy of the uterine muscle which expels it & the hard walls of the birth canal which, threatening to close in, yet pass it thru the ring of the cervix, out. the uterus, the placenta, decide when to thrust it out – & yet, coming forth into the light the child suddenly is, appears to us – an other, recognized as itself, making its own appearance into the world. (*What Matters*, 72)

The association of "mother" with darkness is clearly disturbing to Marlatt, an image she comes back to several times. "Mother is inarticulate dark? / Smothering?" She asks herself in one entry and answers, "No. Get water walk to the kitchen" (*What Matters*, 83).

Later in the text, Marlatt gives us a detailed, probably autobiographical account of the birthgiving of her son, and suddenly, the mother pushes her way forcefully into view. It is not possible to go through this experience (unless one is completely anesthetized, as women generally were, a generation ago), without assuming active maternal identity. A woman's body, fully present, conscious, pushing, blowing, interacting with hospital staff and protocol, protesting against the use of epidural anaesthesia but submitting to it anyway, feeling the helplessness of being strapped onto a birthing table surrounded by hospital staff, and finally, giving her last push before the amazing appearance of dark hair, and a baby's body, a boy, crying, "snuggled in a blanket on my stomach . . . small & perfectly HERE" (*What Matters*, 101) – in this sequence the maternal moves out of the dark into active, conscious daylight.

This passage is followed by a series of entries detailing the duties of caring for a young child, carrying, holding, feeding and changing diapers. Some of these passages seem a bit tedious, but what they do is carefully and precisely outline the formidable activity of mothering, not as unconscious force but as conscious, intentional social practice. Sara Ruddick observes that mothering, like any other professional discipline, involves "establishing criteria for failures and successes, . . . setting priorities [and] identifying the virtues and liabilities the criteria presume" (1980, 77). While traditional literature depicts the mother as either absent or entirely available to meet the demands of the child (or more likely failing miserably at it), Ruddick points out that maternal subjectivity implies both the presence and limitation of the mother's availability to the child, since she must constantly engage with the environment, and make professional choices and judgements in mediating her child's needs with the world around her. By separating the activity of mothering from the mother as symbolic figure, Ruddick is able to isolate maternal subjectivity as historical fact. This is similar to what Marlatt achieves in *What Matters*, except that Marlatt does so with a wealth of image and detail. (*What Matters* was the first literary text I encountered, after the birth of my own children, describing the act of birthgiving in any detail. The impact and sheer pleasure of finding one's experience mirrored in writing for the first time, after complete silence, is indescribable. Marlatt's writing has been groundbreaking in this way for many women. As Brenda Carr claims, Marlatt's writing "opens the horizons of possibility" for women, to imagine and reclaim their territorialized space [1990, 121]).

Despite her declaration of the mother as subject, however, Marlatt continues to be fascinated with the maternal as archetype in her journal entries. Here is a subsequent passage flirting with the Neumann-Jungian image of the mother as vessel, as "eternal feminine": "mother – death as much as life – source of mother fear

– natural realization of a taking for every giving – double-handed mother (*What Matters*, 117). One might ask how it is possible to endure the arduous activity of mothering if one associates it with "death as much as life." Marlatt herself follows this image with an extended passage on her new sense of fear, that this newborn son might die, her sense of helplessness as a mother in protecting this small life. Clearly, it is necessary to move beyond the archetype of mother as womb/tomb in order to delineate the place of the mother as active, intentional, vulnerable subject. This is a question that takes us directly to the narrative concerns of *How Hug a Stone*.

*How Hug a Stone* is a poetic sequence of short, lyrical-documentary prose passages (Marlatt defies definition by genre), describing a trip by the author-narrator with her son, Kit, to England, to visit her lost dead mother's relatives in the hope of finding traces of her: "perhaps i will come to understand my mother," she says in the introduction. Unlike Marlatt's previous quest narratives, which are organized around the question of writing itself and function if anything as anti-narrative in that sense, *How Hug a Stone* proceeds by reclaiming the possibility/ necessity of narrative and generic continuity, here associated also with family and genetic continuity: "without narrative," she writes, "how can we see where we've been? or, unable to leave it altogether, what we come from?" (*How Hug a Stone*, 19) There is a significant shift here away from Marlatt's previous conception of quest as losing oneself in strange terrain, getting lost in order to discover oneself as receiver/maker of that process (with its attendant loneliness), to a more tangible sense of being able to find oneself in relation to the other, whether it be language, landscape or history. Subjectivity no longer depends on a simple throwing off of the past, as for example in this passage, near the end of *What*

*Matters*: "there is only the one immediate, personal salvation, of the psyche, your own, without help since help is maternal/paternal & that is the very caul that must be thrown off. to be born: to MATTER" (*What Matters,* 127).

*How Hug a Stone* breaks with postmodernism and its insistence on the present moment, its emphasis on radical discontinuity with the past, and moves, instead, to a new, revisionary sense of historicity, of looking back and seeing the past with fresh eyes, to paraphrase Adrienne Rich in her classic essay, "When We Dead Awaken: Writing as Re-Vision" (1971). The purpose for this turning to the past, in Rich's version, is not to resurrect tradition or reassert old conceptions of identity and relationship: precisely, as Rich says, "not to pass on a tradition but to break its hold over us" (1971, 1,046). In Marlatt's case, there is the felt need to go back to the place of the lost mother's childhood, to scrutinize location and landscape, remaining relatives and family stories, in order to come to terms with the mother's continuing absence. The shift in emphasis from "In the Month of Hungry Ghosts" to *How Hug a Stone* is striking and instructive: by focussing on the place, the location of the lost mother's childhood, the daughter positions herself maternally in relation to it, as adult woman remembering, calling back forgotten child – much as the narrator promised to do at the end of the former piece, "there mother-daughter, i call you up through the spring ("In the Month of Hungry Ghosts," 83). At the same time, by recognizing the procession of generations in the making up of genetic identity, and linking it with the way historical events continue to be inscribed linguistically in words and speech patterns, Marlatt undercuts the notion of fixed individual identity, making both "mother" and "daughter" moments in an ongoing story of continuity and discontinuity.

Accompanied by her son, furthermore, the narrator is forced

to recognize her own daily relation to him as "mother": caretaker, companion, go-between with the previous generation. The maternal thus moves from archetype to historical reality, from "double-handed," larger-than-life, reified symbol of the Great Mother to active, intentional, human-being-in-flux. One of the sub-themes in this text is Kit's allergic response to the English landscape and the narrator-mother's inability to prevent or undo it. Her sense of maternal helplessness is played out in two different ways, first, as the difficulty of being a mother, of mothering, if she hasn't been adequately mothered herself: "i say the mother-things to him but what do i say to the child in me? who mothers me?" (*How Hug a Stone*, 71). Second, as a recognition that the maternal is part of a larger process of generation, of life itself. As a woman, the speaker can thus call on every living thing, on the life process itself, to sustain her in the impossible task of nurturing her child, of participating in the ongoing, intergenerational struggle to be alive: "the, all-powerful tickle, / gulp, wriggle gulping in the whole world hugged in ecstatic / limit, breath's. nothing still" (*How Hug a Stone*, 74).

Marlatt does not abandon her interest in language. As in the previous texts, the narrative proceeds by a careful listening to the precise elements of perception and signification; here there is an opening out beyond the speaker's personal experience, into the surrounding world. Maps, bits of conversation in several dialects, old stories, remembered Indo-European roots of words, all dot the figurative landscape of this text. It is as though history suddenly floods the consciousness of the narrative, fragmenting and layering it, while at the same time endowing it with a sense of continuity, connectedness, what Mary O'Brien calls female "reproductive consciousness."[12] Here is a characteristic passage: "i see my ghostly child in him, not gone & not quite him, as she in

me, mother, grandmother, grand, full grown we stand in, not for."
This observation is followed by the thought that "earth takes back
what is given, *ghos-ti*, hostly & hostile at one" (*How Hug a Stone*,
49). A separation occurs here between the mother as human, one
figure in a long line of genetically connected human beings, and
the earth as matrix, as the ground on which we stand, by which we
exist, female and male, in our separate, mortal incarnations.

That this is not history in the traditional sense of male-centred,
male-controlled events Marlatt is reconstructing here, but, rather,
a revisionary history, in the feminine, in which the mother (as
human body, mind, memory, feeling, absence, presence) takes
her rightful place beside the daughter, is emphasized in passages
like this one: "the news confirm / my landlady's view of history,
this plot we're in," and goes on to ask, "what if history is simply the
shell we exude for a place to lie in? *all wrapped up*, break out
before it buries us. stories can kill" (*How Hug a Stone*, 51). In a
later passage she elaborates further on the limits of the "old story":

a script that continues to write our parts in the passion we
find ourselves enacting, old wrongs, old sacrifices. & the endless struggle to redeem them, or them in ourselves, our "selves"
our inheritance of words." (*How Hug a Stone*, 73)

Narrative, according to Marlatt, must be released from its allegiance to the sacrificial, killing script of Western culture, with its
"enraged mother at the heart of it: lost" (*How Hug a Stone*, 15),
and become, rather, subjectivity-in-process, "a strategy for survival" (*How Hug a Stone*, 75). Such a release will bring us into the
present moment, not in the alienated, cut-off sense of the
postmodern (having lost both father and mother), but in the
reconnected sense of recognizing oneself (nurtured, parented), in

the larger flux of life: "the enfolded present waits for us to have done with hiding-&-seeking terrors, territories, our obsession with the end of things" (*How Hug a Stone*, 75).

The most striking and powerful pieces in *How Hug a Stone* are those that begin to image the lost, suppressed maternal feminine in Western culture as recoverable reality. In "long after The Brown Day of Bride," the absent mother is pictured, for example, beyond the immediate memory of the speaker's own dead mother, as historical figure, as collective memory, inaccurately sung but nevertheless kept alive in the stories of "Mary Gypsy, Mary of / Egypt, Miriam, Marianne suppressed, become / Mary of the / Blue Veil, Sea Lamb sifting sand & dust, dust & bone" (*How Hug a Stone*, 72). The deliberate echo from H.D.'s *Helen in Egypt* and *Trilogy* here suggests the possibility of constructing an alternative literary genealogy of women's writing, similar perhaps to Sandra Gilbert and Susan Gubar's idea in collecting the *Norton Anthology of Women's Literature*.

Marlatt pushes the image of the bride-mother in this piece past the known "stories about her, versions of history that are versions of her" (*How Hug a Stone*, 73) to the following observation:

> though she comes in many guises she is not a person, she is what we come through to & what we come out of, ground & source. the space after the colon, the pause (between the words) of all possible relation. (*How Hug a Stone*, 73)

That is to say, there is no definitive Person or Idea behind the image of the bride-mother, no originating Mother presiding over history, imprinting her image on a series of secondary maternal figures: "she" is analogous neither to the Christian God nor the Platonic Ideal. If you trace her back to source, what you find is rather the *possibility* of "all relation," which the bride-mother represents in her imaginative and reproductive capacity, her potentiality as life spirit.

In the next piece, "Avebury *awi-spek*, winged from buried (egg," Marlatt turns to the earth itself as source and ground of being, with its "fields of (waves of) renewed green, cloud, light" (*How Hug a Stone*, 74). The circle of ancient stones at Avebury become, in the narrator's delighted eyes, "writing in monumental stones. open . . . to sky (-change)" (*How Hug a Stone*, 75). *"She lives,"* explains the narrator, reading this ancient text, "stands for nothing but this longstanding matter in the grass, settled hunks of mother crust, early Tertiary, bearing the rootholes of palms" (*How Hug a Stone*, 75). What is at the "centre" is "earth, only earth": there is no source of being to be discovered but the process itself, sustaining us with its "old slow pulse," its longstanding "stei-ing power." "how hug a stone" here acquires the moving resonance of grieving for the lost human mother, buried under stone, while simultaneously embracing the life process, its strength and continuity, written so powerfully in the Avebury stones – the process that both gave the mother her power and outlasted her.

The image of the absent mother who returns in the guise of a goddess or mythical dream woman (thus bridging the distance between human mother, earthly ground of being, and universal life spirit),[13] is most powerfully presented in the last piece, "feeding the pigeons," where the narrator describes a profound, personal encounter with this "she," standing at the edge of the sea with her son, Kit, who has recovered from his illness and wants to go home. Here is the passage in full:

& i can do nothing but stand in my sandals & jeans unveiled, beat out the words, dance out names at the heart of where we

are lost, hers first of all, wild mother dancing upon the waves,
wide-wandering dove beat against, & the dance beats with you,
claims of the dead in our world (the fear that binds). i am learning how the small ones live, ruffled neck feathers ripple snake-
like movement of the neck last vestige of dinosaurs: then lift,
this quick wing flap, heart at breast strike up a wild beating,
blood for the climb, glide, rest, on air current, free we want to
be where live things are. (*How Hug a Stone*, 78-79)

This passage is remarkable, both for its lyricism and its extraordinary visionary quality. The "wild mother dancing" powerfully
suggests the generative quality of the cosmos, and the depth of the
narrator's grief and desire for her own lost mother. This imaginative and mythical encounter at the edge of the sea enables the
narrator finally to end her quest, to lay aside her sense of maternal
loss and turn to mother her own son, at last. Together, they
envision flying home to Vancouver, "where live things are," in an
airplane – like birds, with their trace of dinosaur in them, fully
connected to their genetic heritage, past and future, fully alive.

In 1984, Marlatt published her ground-breaking, lyrical essay
on the poetics of language, "musing with mothertongue." In it,
she develops the idea of language itself as matrix, as maternal
body, "a living body we enter at birth, [which] sustains and
contains us" (*Touch to My Tongue*, 45). As such, language does
not displace or replace anything, and therefore is not, as in the
post-Saussurean paradigm, characterized primarily by lack, but
rather by presence, experienced first of all as sound, then as
association, and finally, as dream, imagination, and memory.
Marlatt echoes a traditional association between "the act of
composition" and the "act of birthing" here (*Touch to My
Tongue*, 49), but where the traditional metaphor imaged speech
and artistic creation as alternatives to or displacements of the

physical act of birthgiving, Marlatt sees them as continuous with it. The body, that is to say, is not erased in speech and writing but articulated by it – in direct contrast to the male-centred and anti-maternal linguistic paradigm of, say, Roland Barthes, who claimed that "every narrative (every unveiling of the truth) is a staging of the (absent, hidden or hypostatized) father" (1975, 10), and the writer "someone who plays with his mother's body . . . in order to glorify it, to embellish it, or in order to dismember it" (37). In the imaginative space created by Marlatt, alternatively, the maternal body, the maternal impulse to bring forth, to create, and the writer's impulse to speak, to make sounds, to give birth to the subjective and thus to be born by it, are continuous with one another, and exist interdependently.

This conception of language as mothered, mothering, as truly mother tongue, has far-reaching implications that extend into Marlatt's subsequent writing. If it is possible to image the mother as presence rather than absence, as speaking subject rather than mute object, container, vessel, then it is possible to write the mother story as a story of relationships between existing women, and not just as the orphaned daughter's lament. In the highly erotic lesbian love poems that make up the main text of *Touch to My Tongue*, Marlatt plays with the image of Persephone's return to Demeter from underground, as a metaphor for the lovers' separation through geography and circumstances and return to one another (cf. Williamson 1992, 182). A question we might ask here is, If it is important for women to learn to differentiate themselves from their own mothers, how is it that the Demeter-Kore myth provides a useful paradigm for women's erotic rela-tionships with one another? The answer is perhaps that, in order for women to write themselves into being, to reclaim their lost, territorialized space as women, it is necessary for them to collaborate, to give birth to each other. As Brenda Carr puts it, "If the days of the Lone Ranger are over, it seems that women cannot enter the realm of the symbolic, the realm of cultural and social agency, in solo. [It is in] collaborative action where the culture negatives . . . are re-versed, in the solidarity of 'she-and-she-who-is-singing'" (1990, 121). *Touch to My Tongue* celebrates this collaborative process literally, in its dialogue with Cheryl Sourkes's photocollages (in the same text), and Betsy Warland's companion text, *Open is Broken* (1984). It also works to undo the hierarchical relations inscribed in the traditional heterosexual romance plot (where the wife continues to act in a daughterly relation to her husband, financially dependent and therefore answerable to him), by reversing the roles of daughter and mother in the women's erotic encounter. As Janice Williamson comments, "Daughter becomes Demeter, and mother, Persephone, as the fixed identities of the two lovers slide" (1992, 183). The relational complexities set up by this conflation of narratives invites further study; Williamson's article provides an excellent introduction to the politics of the lesbian erotic in this regard. This sense of collaborative identity-making is a dramatic revision of Marlatt's previous emphasis on the individual psyche's responsibility to create itself, against the pull of parental, particularly maternal, influences.

*Ana Historic: A Novel* celebrates maternal absence/presence in a variety of ways, continuing the concerns set forth in *How Hug a Stone*. The novel begins, again, with the recognition of maternal absence, but in this case the narrator-daughter, Annie, voices her lament in an extended monologue addressed directly to the missing mother, Ina. The mother thus takes her place in the text as listener, as ghost, in the present, as well as in memory. The fear of ghosts, monsters, bears, is played out as a series of remembered childhood fantasies and games: "Who's There? she was whispering. knock knock. in the dark" (*Ana Historic*, 9). As the narrator acknowledges, however, it is not the mother who is monstrous in this narrative but, rather, her enforced absence from public discourse, from self-definition:

there *is* a monster, there is something monstrous here, but it's not you. . . . all the housewives absent, their curlerheads, their still mops on their knees in the aftermath of storm. . . . bathrobe sleeping beauties gone in a trice, a trance, embalmed, waiting for a kiss to wake them when their kids, their men would finally come home . . . suspended out of the swift race of the world. (*Ana Historic*, 24)

Then she adds, "the monstrous lie of it: the lure of absence. self-effacing" (*Ana Historic*, 24). Who was it, the novel asks, that enforced this absence, who promoted this monstrous lie, this seductive script of maternal self-effacement, so violently and forcefully that it was accepted and passed on by an entire society's women? So completely that the narrator herself is drawn to it: "how peaceful i thought, how i longed for it. a woman's place. safe. suspended out of the swift race of the world" (*Ana Historic*, 24). This passage is followed immediately by a description of men's activities, active, physical, domineering, in a logging episode taken from the archive documents, their "mastery. the bold line of it" contrasting sharply to the somnambulance of the women. Who else but the masters, the dominators of history, men, whose actions of violence and conquest have been celebrated publicly, written down, repeated, over and over: "history is the real story the city fathers tell of the only important events in the world. a tale of their exploits hacked out against a silent backdrop of trees" (*Ana Historic*, 28)? Against this official documented history, *Ana Historic* posits a second history, secretive, unspoken, full of gaps and silences, obliquely pointing to the reality of women's lives behind the walls of domesticity, "holes in the story," Annie calls them (*Ana Historic*, 26). In many ways this becomes the project of the novel: to strategize ways of recovering, re-inventing this lost history for women, so that it can be seen fully, experienced, heard.

The plot of *Ana Historic* revolves around Annie's work as a historical researcher (she is also the mother of two children), into the life of Mrs. Richards, a nineteenth-century British-born pioneer woman referred to obliquely in the public records of the Vancouver Archives. Fascinated by the question of what the life of this unnamed, unmarried career woman in a chauvinist pioneer village would have been like, Annie begins to imagine and re-invent her personal life, all the while carrying on an imagined dialogue with her dead mother. "These are not facts but skeletal bones of a suppressed body the story is," Anna tells her, "there is a story here, Ina, i keep trying to get to" (*Ana Historic*, 29). We discover that there is a journal, written by Mrs. Richards's daughter, imagining her mother's girlhood (an analogue of this novel), considered to be "private" and therefore not factual, historical by the archive professionals (*Ana Historic*, 30). Over the course of the novel, Marlatt reclaims and develops this idea of the "ahistoric," the "ana-historic" as the appropriate narrative space for women's fictional stories: because we cannot remember women's lives from the historical record kept about us, we are free to invent them. As Annie says of the factual/fictional Mrs. Richards, "we cannot see her and so she is free to look out at the world with her own eyes, free to create her vision of it" (*Ana Historic*, 30).

The act of imaginatively recreating Mrs. Richards' personal life (whom she names Ana, thus introducing a complicated play of words with Annie, Ina and the concept of the ana-historic), becomes for the narrator a model for remembering and re-constructing the story of her own missing mother. Gradually she builds a portrait for us of Ina, another British-born immigrant, nervously out of place in Canada, timidly trying to live up to male expectations, by suppressing her own needs and desires in the service of husband and children. As the narrator gains greater understanding of her, her rage at being abandoned shifts from the mother to the social structure that kept her bound and eventually drove her to despair, and (it is implied) suicide. Annie's monologue addressed to Ina, the missing mother, turns into a sporadic and often painful dialogue with her. The mother's voice, recovered enough to speak back to her, makes it possible for Annie to remember also other, more pleasurable parts of her life: "now i'm remembering. not dis- but re-membering. putting things back together again, the things that have been split off, set aside. what did it mean to leave behind that body aroused by the feel of hot wind, ecstatic with the smell of sage, so excited i could barely contain myself as we left pines and high-blue eagle sky" (*Ana Historic*, 51). Reaching back into her childhood, to recover the sense of independent sensual pleasure, not dependent on male approval, Annie remembers also how it was replaced during adolescence, covered over, with feminine propriety, "pride on the outside, and on the inside – shame," she recalls (*Ana Historic*, 61).

The lament for the missing mother in this text thus becomes a lament also for the shamed, silenced feminine body, a betrayal perpetuated throughout written, male-dominated history, and reinforced in Annie's own experience at every turn, by her mother's instructions, her father's expectations, the boy's taunts at school: "'cunt,' 'slit,' 'boob' ('you boob, you dumb broad')" (*Ana Historic*, 62). In claiming imaginative reconstruction as a viable tool for (re)writing women's histories, *Ana Historic* moves beyond lament and protest, and through what Annie calls "a monstrous leap of the imagination" (*Ana Historic*, 135) becomes an affirmation of the independent reality of women's lives, in community with one another, instead of marginally situated in relation to men.

Marlatt gives two dramatic and moving examples of such womanly encounters toward the end of the novel. The first is a description of the fictional Jeannie Alexander's nineteenth century birthgiving, attended by women friends, including the re-invented, re-imagined Ana Richards. The account of the birthgiving is interspersed ironically with the description of a Dominion Day boat race, taken from the public archive records – an event considered more noteworthy to the fathers of "history" in this village than the birth of the first pioneer child (*Ana Historic*, 126). The image, the sight of the birthgiving body, becomes a metaphor in Ana's mind for the "mouth speaking flesh," and touching it, she imagines being born from "that place . . . with no known name" to "the country she has come into, the country of her body" (*Ana Historic*, 127). She wishes, instead of coming to it late, as a stranger, an immigrant, she could have been "there from the first. indigene. *ingenuus* (born in), native, natural, free(born) – at home from the beginning" (*Ana Historic*, 127). As in "musing with mothertongue," the maternal body becomes synonymous here, in the woman's speaking voice, with the body of language itself, birthing us into being.

The second event, following immediately after, begins with Annie in animated conversation with a woman friend, Zoe, over cappuccino, who is saying that "the real history of women . . . is unwritten because it runs through our bodies: we give birth to each other" (*Ana Historic*, 132). Through the course of her talk, the two women become romantically interested in one another. Following this episode, we see Annie wildly reconstructing the narratives of Ina and Ana, her mother and alter ego, in her mind, rewriting their unhappy endings, imagining for them the terrifically happy ending she is also trying to construct for herself, a fiction that turns finally into a lesbian, erotic encounter with Zoe. "We give place," writes Marlatt, commenting on this narrative outcome, "giving words, giving birth, to each other – she and me. you" (*Ana Historic*, 153).

Lola Lemire Tostevin, in her reading of the novel, criticizes the ending as "unexpectedly conventional in its utopian vision" (1989, 38). Many women, comments Tostevin, will find "solutions to complex social problems limited if confined to the sexual sphere. . . . Is the displacement of 'phallocentrism' by 'vulvalogocenticism' [sic]," she asks, "sufficient" – or does difference based on gender and sexuality merely reproduce the revolutionary potential of feminism within patriarchal terms? (1989, 38). Tostevin's criticism strikes me as reductive, given the complexity of Marlatt's agenda in *Ana Historic*. By creating a narrative space for those women's experiences that were omitted or distorted in the traditional patriarchal script – including the experience of adolescent female desire and its suppression, maternal desperation passed down from one generation to the next, the amazing, powerful experience of birthgiving, and the solidarity of women acting in community – Marlatt has written a story that very naturally also contains the possibility of women's erotic encounter with one another. Marlatt's ending, far from being "prescriptive," celebrates what Adrienne Rich has called the "lesbian continuum," which includes such various and vital encounters between women as, to paraphrase Rich, a woman suckling her child, two women sharing a laboratory, and a woman dying at ninety, touched and handled by women (1990, 302-03). Marlatt's novel, I would argue, far from reinvesting in traditional, binary definitions of gender, opens out onto the rich variety of (historically suppressed) differences between and among women, where the maternal and the sexual assume their place as part of women's experience and not the symbolic whole.

# These Our Grand-mothers

Jovette Marchessault's *Like a Child of the Earth,*
*Mother of the Grass* and *White Pebbles in the Dark Forests*

Jovette Marchessault's recently translated novel trilogy, *Like a Child of the Earth* (1988), *Mother of the Grass* (1989) and *White Pebbles in the Dark Forests* (1990), reads like fireworks, one colourful explosion of narrative expectation after another. "My origin is celestial and I was born in Montreal during the thirties," declares the narrator in the opening sentence, thus announcing a double narrative structure that informs the work as a whole, one strand of which is visionary, extra-terrestrial, and shamanic, and the other, realistic in the conventional sense. This double structure allows Marchessault to explore an alternative vision that is not tied to Western cultural practice but, rather, draws on her Aboriginal ancestry and her own psychic experience, which in turn radically politicizes the "realistic" story being told. Maxine Hong Kingston uses a similar technique in *The Woman Warrior* (1976) to describe her experience of growing up as the daughter of Chinese-American immigrants in California. Here is an effective model for women to

**75**

explore, re-imagine and reclaim the female heritage that was lost to them through colonization and immigration, and at the same time to critique current social and narrative practices that reiterate that process.

Lorna Irvine, in *Sub/Version*, describes women's writing as typically double, split between the requirements of public, male-centred discourse and female desire (Irvine 1986, 3-19). This doubleness, argues Irvine, echoing Lacan, implies a split within the self, an unavoidable duplicity in the female speaking subject. Irvine envisions this split as a dynamic and subversive force in women's fiction, able to break open conventional ways of seeing and knowing. Julia Kristeva and Alice Miller have similarly demonstrated that female desire, and the female imaginary, when taken seriously as the existential, and cultural, ground of women's experience, becomes a site of healing, both for the split female subject and for the structures that support it (Kristeva 1980; Miller 1990). Such healing often does not occur without great internal conflict, leading to separation and/or transformation; sometimes it can lead to death. Kristeva talks about the borderline of psychosis that must be risked and negotiated in order for the suffering subject to reclaim her experience from the "void" of the unnameable (1980, x). Carol P. Christ describes suicide as one of the possible tragic results if personal awakening in women is not accompanied by adequate social support (1980, 27-40). Marchessault's preoccupation with the healing not only of the speaking subject but of the planet as a whole means that the entire universe must be called upon to witness the spectacle of ongoing violence, which perpetuates the splitting of consciousness and experience, and to participate in its reuniting through recognition and protest.

While most contemporary writers of Western European ancestry have scrupulously avoided the question of "origins" in writing because of its Christian-metaphysical implications, Marchessault leaps without hesitation into this cosmic terrain. At the end of the first volume, *Like a Child of the Earth*, the narrator, Jeanne (we find out her name in the third volume), exhorts us to break through our customary amnesia and recollect our magical, celestial origins:

Women, do not be stunned. Men, do not be stunned. Instead, take your throat between your two hands and force yourself to spit up a river of sleeping pills. Make connections! Interweave yourselves! Commit yourselves to memory in the time of your childhood, in the time of your permanent emotion. Tear yourselves down to the weft of your being and rally all of your memories. Memories in your cells, memories in your head, memories in your heart, in your soul, and in the infinitely mercurial memories of your spirit. (*Like a Child of the Earth*, 166)

She then takes us on a journey to "remember" her own blissful pre-existence among the stars, and subsequent "fall," through the ear and mouth of the great She-Wolf in the sky, "descending straight down like a spit from the sun" (*Like a Child of the Earth*, 176) into human birth as a girl child.

Gloria Orenstein describes Marchessault's birth narrative, here (and in the later, more overtly lesbian "A Lesbian Chronicle from Medieval Quebec"), as a feminist-lesbian revisioning of the classic hero myth, in which a male child is imagined to have divine or noble origins, who is abandoned at birth, raised in exile by humble people, and eventually called to his heroic destiny as the leader of his people through certain events. In Marchessault's version, says Orenstein, "For the first time in its long history from Sappho to Adrienne Rich, from Renee Vivien to Rita Mae Brown, an

extraterrestrial heroine makes her appearance in lesbian literature, heralding the advent of a new myth of origins for woman-
identified women" (Orenstein 1987, 188-89). The moment of
her "sacred fall" (*Like a Child of the Earth*, 173) also re-enacts
the traditional Christian-classical story of the hero's fall from
heaven, with these significant differences: this fall is not precipi-
tated by pride, or hubris, as in the case of Lucifer and Icarus, but,
rather, the heroine's parent stars rejecting her, "pushing" her into
generation. "That is what it is all about," laments the narrator,
remembering her life prior to earthly conception, "– it is about
rejection. On earth we speak of birth, but the word birth is a word
which we have borrowed from the void, from the super-void. . . .
They were going to reject me. They were going to turn me away
once again. They were going to double-lock the door and throw
me out into the generation of fathers" (*Like a Child of the Earth*,
167). The fall is thus in itself, quite apart from the intentions of the
heroine, a begetting, a birthing, a letting go, and not a separate,
contrary moment from creation, as in the Christian/classical
view. For Marchessault, the separation that occurs in the moment
of conception and birth, and the ongoing separation into individuality – albeit traumatic and filled with "rejection" for the child – are
simply part of the reproductive process, and deeply connected to
the physical reality of the cosmos, that is envisioned here as a kind
of primal maternal body.

What is striking here on the theme of "origins" is both the
physicality of the universe, and its personal, feminine aspect. The
stars are not an abstract metaphor for disembodied spirits in a
male-defined heaven, nor are they alienated blobs of gravitational
matter floating around in empty space. "The Milky Way," for
Marchessault, is a physical place, best described in personal,
experiential terms, with fields to walk in, and sunsets to paint. It is,

furthermore, deeply resonant with the image of a woman, the Grandmother. "I heard the music of an ancient dance issuing from the void," the narrator tells us, remembering the moment just before her fall, "or, more precisely, coming from the womb of the Grandmother. Her over-flesh, over-earth, over-sea womb was coming toward us, breaking its moorings" (*Like a Child of the Earth*, 166). It is difficult, I think, for readers steeped in Western thought to appreciate the implications of this vision, and the radical challenge it offers to non-Native, dualistic thinking: there isn't a fall into conception, there isn't a fall away from Idea, or Word, or Spirit, into the body, there isn't a fall from father sky to mother earth. There is rather a passage, a birth-giving, from one state of physical/spiritual being into another, through the celestial body of the She Wolf, her ear canal, her mouth, helped along with a swat from the paws of the presiding Great She-Bear of the sky. Our biggest mistake, according to Marchessault, is forgetting our physical/spiritual connections to the cosmos, and its formidable reproductive, regenerative power. "It was an absolutely new beginning," exclaims the narrator at the end of *Like a Child of the Earth*, "and you will never make me believe that everything is motivated by the unconscious or the subconscious. I say that the whole source of motivation is metaphysical, that it falls in a direct line from the Great Spirit and from the Great She-Bear's breasts, with every kind of admirable sign, miracle, and mutation, and it is this unique source which impregnates us" (*Like a Child of the Earth*, 175).

Mary Crow Dog, in her recent autobiography, *Lakota Woman*, offers the following explanation of the North American Native visionary practice, and describes what happened in a ceremony that was banned by the American government in the nineteenth century, and revived on a Sioux reservation in 1974:

Dreams and visions are very important to us, maybe more important than any other aspect of Indian religion. I have met Indians from South and Central America, from Mexico and from the Arctic Circle. They all pray for visions, they are all "crying for a dream," as the Sioux call it. Some get their visions from fasting for four days and nights in a vision pit on a lonely hilltop. Others get their visions fasting and suffering during the long days of the Sun Dance, gazing at the blinding light in the sky. The Ghost Dancers went around and around in a circle, chanting until they fell down in a swoon, leaving their own bodies, leaving the earth, wandering along the Milky Way and among the stars. When they woke up they related what they had seen. Some found "star flesh" in their clenched fists, and moon rocks, so it is said. (Crow Dog 1991, 98-99)

The mythic visionary nature of the universe, in other words, is experienced by its practitioners, through dreams and rituals, as literally, physically, demonstrably real. Crow Dog describes how the missionary superintendent at Pine Ridge Sioux Indian reserve tried to discredit Native medicine men during the 1940s by "exposing" their rituals. The leading medicine man, Horn Chips, was asked to perform a *yuwipi* (magic) ceremony for a group of white observers, who supervised the preparations. "To the disappointment of the watching missionaries," relates Crow Dog, "the mystery sparks appeared out of nowhere and the gourds flew around the superintendent's head. The result was that many Christian Indians went back to the old Lakota religion" (Crow Dog, 211). Within the North American Native mythic paradigm, then, the Western dichotomy between science and the imagination does not make any sense. Magical events are observable and performable, and therefore "scientifically" true. But in order for them to occur in the first place there has to be imagination and belief on the part of the participants. There do not appear to be any inherent limits to the kinds of imaginative/experiential connections that can be made between individuals and the universe through visionary practice; the only limits stem from lack of intention and focus in the believers themselves.

Nuclear physicist Fred Alan Wolf, author of *Taking the Quantum Leap* (1981) and *The Eagle's Quest* (1991), argues that the newest insights of nuclear quantum physics correlate to a remarkable degree with ancient shamanic teachings. Heisenberg's famous uncertainty principle, which announced that it is impossible to determine the location and the momentum of a particle simultaneously, shattered Western belief in the material certainty of the world we live in. Determinism and causality, the cornerstones of Western science, no longer hold in the quantum universe. According to the new quantum physics, explains Wolf, electrons do not actually have mass and therefore do not occupy identifiable space. They are rather tendencies, concepts, ideas, probabilities:

We can't even specify at any moment what the condition of reality is because of the uncertainty principle; instead we have probable possibilities. These possible particles represent a cloud of possibilities in which the actual particle is somehow enfolded but is not actually present as an object would be, like an ash tray or cup. . . . Quantum physics tells us there isn't really any such thing as a particle, only possible particles." (Wolf, as cited in Leviton 1992, 52)

The virtuality of matter throws the focus back on the observer, and particularly the observer's intent. Our intent influences the materialization of electrons out of their virtual state of infinite probability. It is therefore our belief that makes reality appear in a given manifestation. "The observer effect," argues Wolf, "is probably the most important thing we've ever discovered in terms of relating magic to physical reality. If you take quantum mechanics as it's presently understood, that's magic. You have a cloud of possibilities that suddenly manifest into one actuality" (Wolf, as cited in Leviton 1992, 53).

Wolf argues further that in order to become more focussed in our intent, more consciously "cocreative" with the universe, we must integrate its feminine aspect into our nature. "I learned that the magic in me was in my feminine spirit, in my reawakened feminine core," he explains. "You have to understand both elements of the mythic reality of yourself, the male and female, in order to portray either of those realities in your life" (Wolf, as cited in Leviton, 55). This statement can be interpreted in the Jungian sense as a need for psychic integration of opposites within the self, but the implications for constructing a contemporary cosmology that will accurately reflect human experience are equally radical and profound. (Wolf, incidentally, and perhaps not surprisingly, has turned to shamanism in recent years as a more profound and satisfying imaginative paradigm of how the universe works than the one offered by quantum physics [Leviton 1992, 55]).

Feminist poet Libby Scheier, in her poetry collection, *SKY*, expresses a similar concern for recovering the feminine aspect of the universe. Her poems represent a powerful revisioning of the alienated cosmos of Western science, in connection with her personal healing process. (She was raped as a young girl.) In order to be whole, Scheier's poems suggest, we must reclaim the "lost" parts of ourselves from outer space, from the abstract, empty space we imagine "out there," which is really a projection of our own split-off, alienated selves. Through personal healing, we can begin to experience the universe in its nurturing aspect, as a feminine, maternal, caring body. Here is her image of "sky," as a kind of grand, celestial womb:

be that as it may
sky's been kind to us, a mother muse
blue, pervasive, like sound through silence

. . .

we are inside sky,
like we were inside mother,
can we remember how limitless we felt? (Scheier 1990, 19)

Marchessault's interest in "origins" clearly stems from this same interest in envisioning a holistic and woman-affirming cosmology. "Two questions torment us – the question of origins and beginning and the question of the final outcome. Everything else is just padding and a way of passing time" (*Like a Child of the Earth*, 121). This statement, if we are to take Marchessault's vision seriously, must be read as a political protest against our modernist sense of alienation from the past, the universe, and our human power as imaginative, creative, (re)generative beings, and not as a lapse into essentialism or escape from historicity.[14] Out of this alienation, suggests Marchessault, arises our contemporary inability to imagine the future. We might think of Margaret Laurence's famous dictum at the end of *The Diviners*: "Look ahead into the past, and back into the future, until the silence," as a similar reminder to become reconnected to the (re)generative process that carries us through history (Laurence 1974, 370). As Gloria Orenstein explains, referring to Marchessault's fictions:

All the potential for evolution and mutation is stored in the human memory of our cells. . . . Both the invisible energies of plants and minerals as well as the invisible genetic material of all women who have lived in past ages and in all incarnations constitute the inherited living matter of our psycho-cellular beings, the prima materia of imagination and creation. (Orenstein 1987, 187)

Perhaps the most distinctive feature of Marchessault's imaginative vision is the place of animals and plants in it. While many contemporary feminist writers have begun to express their concern for the environment in a variety of ways, including the revival of goddess imagery, protesting against images of violence toward women and the body, and revisioning metaphors of earth and landscape, it is really Aboriginal writers, drawing on the shamanic tradition, who have most successfully articulated reverence for the plant and animal worlds. In traditional Aboriginal terms, animals and plants do not hold an inferior position to humans in the universal structure of creation. On the contrary, animals, birds, plants, fish, all hold special, sacred knowledge that can help human beings, and that, if anything, demonstrates their greater connectedness to the Great Universal Spirit. Mary Crow Dog talks about the meaning of animals to the Aboriginal imagination in her autobiography. Here is her description of (her husband) Leonard Crow Dog's stay in prison:

Leonard told me he communicated with birds outside his window or in the yard. They seemed to him to be spirit messengers and they cheered him up. Once a crow perched on his windowsill and that made him feel good. He thought it was a Crow Dog spirit come to visit him. Another time it was a yellowhammer which to him represented the Peyote Church [peyote is the hallucinogenic herb used in ritual ceremonies]. During a parole hearing he saw two eagles through the window circling in the clouds and he took this for a good sign. He always felt the presence of the spirits, even when he was in the hole. "Tunkashila is watching over me," he told me one time. "I have a hot line to the Great Spirit. I got a built-in amplifier for talking to Tunkashila. (Crow Dog, 235)

The identity of plants and animals, that is to say, is not recognizable in discrete, abstractly defined, objective categories, as in Western science, but rather must be understood mythically. Every living being is connected to every other living being through the universal life spirit. Each reflects the reality of every other being back to them. There is no "metaphysical" realm outside or beyond the physical. Animal and god, body and spirit, are inextricably and organically linked through the life process, and capable of infinite permutation. Separating the divine from the bestial, and the eternal from the temporal, the way we have done in Western metaphysics, is an act of violence that leads to sickness and death in individual creatures and in the universal organism. In order to understand "difference" in the physical world we must also be able to recognize its intricate interconnectedness.[15]

Marchessault's vision of a sacred cosmos in which animals and plants preside along with rocks and stars is mythical in a way that is foreign to Western thinking. However, contemporary Western concern over the threatened environment has brought us to a vision of the planet as a vastly interconnected and interdependent ecosystem, not unlike Marchessault's cosmos. In her book *The Chalice and the Blade*, Riane Eisler criticizes the "dominator" model, which has characterized social thinking throughout Western history, including modern science, and offers a more egalitarian, interdependent model, which she calls the "partnership" mode. The latter, she argues, is a much more accurate way of describing effective evolutionary development than "survival of the fittest," and she offers us a way of thinking about future as open-ended and life-affirming, as opposed to the dead-end approach that is currently operative in much of the world (Eisler 1988). The general trend of the new science, she explains, which includes "chaos" theory and feminist scholarship as well as quantum physics, is to develop more egalitarian, empathic, integrative, caring approaches to research and knowledge, no longer "directed toward the domination of nature or of humanity as part of nature" (Hillary Rose 1983: cited in Eisler 1988, 191). The kinds of relationships we foster between men and women, Eisler argues further, are crucial to the success of the partnership model, since it is the oppression of women and their connection to the reproductive process that lies at the core of the dominator mode (1988, 202-23).

Marchessault's narrative of celestial origin, with its grand figures of the Great She-Bear in the sky, and the great cosmic Grandmother behind her, suggests a revival of the Aboriginal shamanic vision, in dialogue with feminism and the "new science." Her images offer a critique of Western cultural practice, and challenge it in mythic and revisionary terms. Marchessault's novels passionately protest the objectification of the natural world and the degradation of the woman's body. The awakening of consciousness, Marchessault's fictions declare, involves recovering a magical connection to the universe through memory and imagination. Such a connection presupposes a basic reverence for the mother: as matrix, as generative, intelligent, nurturing body, as independent woman, as totem animal, as universal consciousness. Like other feminist writers, Marchessault laments the absence/oppression/murder/silencing of the maternal body and maternal subject in Western culture – a violent suppression imposed on Aboriginal cultures in the last few centuries, as it was violently imposed on pagan Europe before that.

Because her memory of a former culture in which the mother was honoured and celebrated is relatively recent, Marchessault is able to reclaim the mother story with less irony than most non-Aboriginal writers. On the other hand, her sense of literary production as a mode of bringing the mother back into social discourse is deeply informed by the irony of participating in Western narrative structures, with their misogynist, colonizing history. Here is a passage from *White Pebbles in the Dark Forests*, which describes the narrator's difficulty in holding on to this dynamic double edge:

Sometimes I tell myself that it is pointless to try to tell this story. I do not have enough strength for this work. And anyway, does literature have the right to get involved with miracles? Literature, with its critical violence and its need for rational, historical proofs, which it loves to heap up and stir till it makes you sick to your stomach. Writing is like waving a sword in the air, like having a fit of hysterics in the belly of a carp. But all the same . . . if only once literature could think beyond its permitted limits. After all, literature is Mother, a vital energy which pours itself out into the world. Oh Mother Literature, I implore you, I beg you on bended knees to protect your little girl on these sterile plains which extend from book to book, these steppes which are increasingly dangerous to cross. (*White Pebbles in the Dark Forests*, 9)

*Like a Child of the Earth*, the first of the novels, which marked Marchessault's literary debut in Canada, is structured as a journey quest, depicting the narrator's travels around "Native North America" in the "belly of a dog," a Greyhound bus, with her friend Francine. As we follow them from one dirty bus depot to another, the narrator shares her dreams and observations of the landscape with us. Her purpose, she tells us, is to acquaint herself with the Native North American geography, in order to "appropriate" and "annex" it imaginatively for herself and for Aboriginal people, in defiance of Christopher Columbus and several hundred years of European colonization. The narrator's odyssey takes us through a series of geographical and imaginary landscapes, ranging from Montreal to New York to rural New Mexico. Along the way we encounter the ghosts of a variety of characters who have influenced the North American cultural imagination, from Jack Kerouac to Columbus to King Kong. We also catch a glimpse of Atlantis, which, Marchessault claims, is the sunken continental bridge that once linked Africa with the Americas, and our only existing explanation for "the analogies, echoes, and extensions between the fauna and the flora of the Azores, Madeira, the Canary Islands, Cape Verge, the Antilles, and Central America" (*Like a Child of the Earth*, 37). Marchessault's reclaiming of the mythical island as geological fact makes it possible for her to bridge opposing cultures and continents. It also allows her to ground her sense of the imaginary as another version of the real in the landscape itself. She is thus able to avoid the pitfalls of writing from the point of view of cultural otherness, while turning the colonizing project back on itself.

The quest ends with her vision/memory of celestial origins, as described above, and the experience of sliding into human birth. The journey motif thus circles around, geographically and in time; there is not a linear narrative line from "away" to "home," as in Homer's *Odyssey*, or from "home" to "away," as in *Moby Dick* and *Huckleberry Finn*.[16] Rather, by the end of the novel, the entire North American continent and the universe itself come to be recognized imaginatively as home by the narrator. The body of the mother is, analogously, imaged not as the cataclysmic beginning and end of the story, the traumatic womb/tomb of the self, but rather as universal, generative matrix that makes possible the birth and growth of individual human (and therefore universal) consciousness.

*Mother of the Grass*, Marchessault's second novel, depicts the narrator's childhood, growing up in a "Catholic tribe," her extended family, on the banks of a river on the outskirts of Montreal, and her subsequent move with them to the "Land of Permanent Sacrifice," in a poverty-stricken area of the inner city. The narrative focus shifts, significantly, away from the cosmic and global terrain of the first novel, with its endless journeying possibilities, to the more limited, socially defined arena of the family. There is a corresponding shift in style away from the exclamatory mysticism of the first novel to a kind of mythic realism. Here are two passages, taken from the opening chapters of the two novels, to illustrate this shift:

When I am thirty, I can, if I stick out my tongue and take a thousand precautions, a thousand baby steps, while fluttering my wings, suck from the breasts of the Great She-Bear, she who lives in the white land of the tree-eater. When I have satisfied my thirst, I cover the ashes of my face, now the colour of cornstraw, and return into myself. But if, standing on the edge of horror and cold, I feel I am threatened, I make the sign of the cross and strike the flint and steel to light the little suns which I hide in my armpits and so warm and soothe myself again. (*Like a Child of the Earth*, 7)

In those days, we lived beside the river. We were my grandmother, my mother, my father, and my grandmother's second husband. We lived as a tribe, in a great congregation of nerve cells and blood cells. And we lived with eyes in the back of our heads to catch sight of the prophets of calamity with their volcanic eruptions of rumour. Black clouds, grey novenas, and violet scapulars. This tribe of Catholics, head over heels in the holy water font! Bad news spurting everywhere, distributed free by the waves, by everyone, by the newspapers. (*Mother of the Grass*, 7)

The point is not, I think, that Marchessault abandons her shamanic vision in favour of realism, but rather that, having established its magical possibilities in narrative terms, the shamanic becomes a frame for what follows, a point of view from which to critique Western narrative conventions, including their investment in the colonized, industrialized, Christianized family. A vivid and central character in *Mother of the Grass* is the narrator's grandmother, a tragic-heroic maternal figure who exerts great imaginative influence on her granddaughter. Her stature clearly derives from the cosmic Grandmothers in *Like a Child of the Earth*, and her strength represents an important challenge to the Western tradition with its maternal absences. As a "character," she is certainly the most influential figure in Marchessault's trilogy.

The Grandmother is depicted, through her granddaughter's eyes, as an artist of great skill and imagination. Her piano music, recalls the narrator, was "at one with the Earth, with its underground springs, its caverns, its earthworms, its thunder lizards, with germination, that vegetal and mineral epiphany ripening in the bomb of a volcano or the palm of an ice floe. Grandmother's music was full to the brim" (*Mother of the Grass*, 14). The Grandmother is a powerful storyteller, mixing Catholic superstition with personal fantasy and shamanic lore, and animating the narrator's childhood imagination with vivid, life-affirming images. "No matter what or whom she spoke about," remembers the narrator, "her speech sparked an immediate pleasure throughout my entire body. Her stories were almost always about flesh and blood creatures, and it didn't matter if the flesh and blood was vegetable, mineral, or animal. What she knew and understood about each and every thing was a recognition which was life-giving, which injected vitality. Listening to her was for me to listen to the collective voice of every living thing" (*Mother of the Grass*, 18). Later we see her painting glorious, magical pictures of hens. The maternal, in Marchessault's view, is not divorced from the powers of the creative imagination or in competition with it, as in the Western European tradition, but at one with it. Mother and artist are literally the same thing, both participating joyfully in the (re)productive spirit of the universe.

The Grandmother is equally at home playing games with the children and speaking her mind about politics. "You should have seen her leap on the ice with both feet together," exclaims the narrator, remembering her skating on the river, "with a spring in her arms and legs. . . . Dizzying pirouettes! Jumping like a frog when her skate caught a rough patch in the ice. Gliding through the air with the wind in her face. Snowploughing to a stop" (*Mother of the Grass*, 20). During the war, her second husband and the narrator's father are employed at the munitions factory. They talk very little, afraid to think about the death they manufacture daily with their hands, afraid to think of the war ending and their jobs along with it. The Grandmother, on the other hand, the narrator tells us, "brought her rage out of the cupboard; . . . she banged her fists on the table and got up to spit on the stove, restraining herself so that she didn't break everything in the kitchen. Grandmother had no desire to temporize or compromise with the war. That slaughter was her living nightmare" (*Mother of the Grass*, 23). The men look at her sceptically, and call her crazy for wanting to "change the world." The narrator child, however, understands and identifies with her revolutionary spirit, which is

**91**

the other side of her playfulness. She recognizes the way both are part of the life-giving, creative force that make her the (Grand)mother in the first place.

The Grandmother is also a healer. In the spring she collects herbs, which grow plentifully in the fields and ditches of Montreal. "In the heavens," the narrator tells us, "the Mother of the Grass was creating her flora, weaving without haste all kinds of herbs. . . . The Mother of the Grass was giving birth to her daughters of vegetation, her daughters venerated in the Spring sky" (*Mother of the Grass*, 24). The "Mother of the Grass," we find out elsewhere, is a mythical reference to the moon (*Mother of the Grass*, 154). She is also what Western readers would identify as Primavera, goddess of spring, and Demeter, goddess of harvest. In fact, it is interesting that, while the goddess figures in the Greek myths are differentiated by function and location, all are conflated in Native mythology in the figure of the Mother. This is one answer to the fragmentation of the feminine psyche in Western culture.[17]

Marchessault follows her mythic depiction of spring with a list of the healing herbs, and their uses, collected by the Grandmother. It is a wild catalogue of names, creating a sense of visionary splendour, in epic fashion. Unlike the lists of names we're accustomed to in the Western tradition, these herbs do not have official names, imposed on them institutionally, nor even folk names passed on through popular usage. Rather, they are referred to by their healing properties, available to anyone who recognizes them and is willing to go out and pick them in common fields and ditches:

[The Mother of the Grass] was giving birth to herbs which aid the birthing of complete babies or of fetuses. To affectional herbs, for every affection, respiratory, cardiac, and intestinal as well as the other kinds. To herbs for pain, pains all over, articular pain, pains of anger, pains of patience, pains in the pit of the stomach and in the heights of the heart. And to herbs for predicaments, for the bending of rules. To herbs for children, for chilblains, for convulsions, for seizures. To herbs all golden from the light which is organized within them. [And so on.] (*Mother of the Grass*, 25)

That is to say, the "language" by which plants are named is the language of the body's response to them. It is a language that cannot be spoken in words alone, and therefore cannot be transmitted in books but only by intimate interaction with the herbs themselves, a "hands on" knowledge passed on personally, from mother to daughter.

We might compare Marchessault's catalogue with Morag Gunn's list of common weed names in *The Diviners*: "Curly Pondwood / Silver Hairgrass / Old Witch Grass / Prostrate Pigweed / Nightflying Catchfly / Queen-of-the-Meadow . . . Povertyweed / Staggerwort / Devil's Paintbrush" (*The Diviners*, 333). Morag and her friend Tom exchange "glances of glee and mutual appreciation" over the list, which Morag has found in an unnamed "weed and wildflower" book. Though Laurence does not elaborate, we assume Morag's amusement derives from the unexpected, rich imaginative landscape inscribed in the names. Set next to Marchessault's catalogue, we can see how deeply Laurence's list is embedded in the particular cultural history of medieval Europe, with its heritage of witches and faeries and devils, filtered through the Christian dual categories of good and evil. "With us, knowing the weeds isn't essential to survival," reflects Morag, "at least not any more and not yet," pointing to the possibility (and perhaps necessity) of reviving the lost art of healing through herbs, which was violently eradicated in Europe during the witch hunts that marked the beginning of modern, male-dominated "science" (Daly 1978; Read 1990). For Marchessault, on the other hand, the knowledge of weeds as useful to human survival is as recent as the memory of the Grandmother, treating the ills and woes of the many men and women who come through her kitchen, begging for treatment.

Everywhere in the text, Marchessault inserts mythical references to the Mother. The grandchildren, who accompany the Grandmother in her search for herbs, discover caves in the forest that they explore with curiosity and trepidation. "Upon entering the cave," writes Marchessault, "we altered our identities along the way, like a crystal which becomes a diamond. Who were we? Who were we really? Were we emeralds in their rocky wombs or explorers or gold prospectors cast out from the hard, sharp matter of a great American city? Or were we children of the earth in search of a universal Mother, a mother hidden in these subterranean galleries, a mother long since forgotten because her black, acid, gleaming eyes were like those of insects or of fish with beautiful spotted bellies and fins sharpened and polished by the wear and tear and beating of the water of the deeps?" (*Mother of the Grass*, 49). Unlike Neumann's Great Mother, whose function is mainly that of birthgiving, of "vessel," centred in adult (male) interests, Marchessault's "universal Mother" evokes awe on her own behalf, and demands the ego's surrender to childlike imaginative wonder, wherein identities are not fixed but are capable of magical transformation.

Phyllis Webb, in a recent interview, has observed that "the big paradigm shift in our culture right now is the feminist shift, the shift into the realization of the feminine point of view, experience and theory. . . . The other, of course," she adds, "is the environmental shift, where we, in order to survive, must change our vision from centering on the human-centered to the animal- and environment-centered view of the world. That is what Olson in fact posited in 'Projective Verse,' that our egos must shrink" (Webb/ Kamboureli 1991-92, 28). It is interesting to note that, in Marchessault's vision, this shrinking and letting go does not involve self-flagellation and renunciation, as in the Christian and Buddhist traditions, but rather the recovery of imaginative playfulness and a sense of wonder.

Song Four, entitled "The Cart before the Horse," describes the forced emigration of the narrator's family, including the Grandmother and her second husband, due to post-war unemployment, to Montreal's poverty-stricken inner city. This is the Land of Permanent Sacrifice, scathingly depicted by the narrator, who endures young adolescence here, as a sea of violence and despair. The fathers in this working-class and welfare neighbourhood are listless and unmotivated, for the most part, except when eating and drinking or beating their children. The mothers, on the other hand, are active and exhausted, worked to the bone, "rubbing, scrubbing, cleaning, washing, drying, hanging up the clothes on the line to the telephone pole, scrubbing again, tidying, wrinkling their noses because they smelt piss or shit, pulling back the sheets, peeling potatoes," and on and on (*Mother of the Grass*, 79), in an endless litany of unacknowledged domestic tasks. Marchessault's celebration of the Mother and her (re)creative power clearly has its dark underside: the recognition that "motherhood" as practised in the Western nuclear family is deeply oppressive to women.

Divinity is present in the Land of Permanent Sacrifice, not as the resplendent "Mother of the Grass," pouring out her blossoms on the world, but rather a stern, reproachful God the Father, "a kind of Jack the Ripper," says Marchessault, "who waved his dagger and brandished his whip. The God of back alleys, the God of prisons, hangings, the God of the Mounted Police" (*Mother of the Grass*, 78). The mothers, in contrast to the Grandmother with her artistic and healing powers, rub and scrub and entertain murderous thoughts of their too many children:

I love my children and the Good Lord. I have another one on the way. I'm going to bring it on, throw it down the toilet or bury it in the garbage can. Or maybe it would be better to let it be born and then strangle it if it's a girl. I could strangle her with my bare hands and look her straight in the face. Maybe that's the only way to point her in another direction, toward something else. Sometimes, when I look at the kids, I'd love to push them back into my body and cross them off the supreme voter's list. (*Mother of the Grass*, 79)

Song Four is a kind of scream, a cry of despair, for all the mothers who have experienced the oppressive aspects of "motherhood," as practised in Western culture under the shadow of the Father. It is also a scream of outrage for the daughters, who are stripped of adequate role models and who turn against the passivity of their mothers:

The silent monologue of the mommies in their kitchens, their kennels. Mama, mommies, why didn't you speak up more? Why, I am asking you. I will go on asking you forever. Miserable mucky mama! Miserable mucky mama, you should have screamed out loud. Damn you, mama, you accomplice! Damned sticky, drowned, walled-up, flattened-out mama, why? Why, I ask you! You were afraid. You were always afraid. You were always afraid of someone or something, it didn't matter what. You were always afraid of words, afraid of the big penis in words. (*Mother of the Grass*, 83)

Song Four culminates in a dramatic, desperate act by the granddaughter. Pushed beyond endurance by the awfulness of life in the Land of Permanent Sacrifice, she impulsively turns on the gas in the middle of the night, and goes back to bed. Her act of murdering the family is intercepted, however, as we find out in Song Five, by the Grandmother, with her keen sense of smell. Both the Grandmother and mother are shocked, horrified, though the Grandmother in her wisdom knows enough not to argue with the girl or remonstrate, nor to report the incident to the men. The mother takes her to Catholic confession the next morning, but there is no repentance in her: "No! I said it all by myself, my lips unsealed – no. No! No! I was not sorry. There was not a single ounce of regret in my body, nothing but crystal, black salt, and diamond chips crystallized in the unifying light of revolt. It boiled in my head and my path divided. I could not ask for pardon or bow my back as far as that. No! No! No!" (*Mother of the Grass*, 101). It is at home, later, in bed with her mother and grandmother, that she finds absolution through crying: "My mother was crying tear after tear; then my grandmother, then me. The three of us in one bed, absolving ourselves of all guilt, curing ourselves of my gesture of death. I love you, my mothers. I love you to death. I love you to life. . . . I love you, my mothers" (*Mother of the Grass*, 102).

Gloria Orenstein comments on this passage as follows:

It is her unusual use of the plural in this line "I love you, my mothers" that illuminates the original interpretation of the meaning of mothers in Jovette Marchessault's work. This concept of the plurality of mothers refers to her entire biological matrilineage as well as to all her spiritual, natural, and mythic mothers. For the mothers of her rebirth are manifold. In *La Mère des herbes [Mother of the Grass]* they are at once the ancient mammals of the Neolithic caves, the protective angels of her childhood, Plant Mother, the Indian-Magus Keteri Tekakwita who performs miracles, her mother, grandmother, neighbour Belle Beatrice, and all the mother forces of the universe – the sun, the moon, the plants, the earth, and the river (Orenstein 1987, 187-88).

The child-narrator finds absolution and healing, not through repentance for her rebellious, angry act, but through commiseration with the mothers. There is no expulsion of the feminine/ maternal subject in order to stabilize the society of the fathers. Rather, there is the possibility of community among women through their shared grief and love.

   While the murderous impulse of the child is not condoned by the narrator, the anger and frustration it represents, the sense of outrage in daughters against the continual sacrifice required of their mothers, is fully acknowledged, made present, in the text. So is the murderous impulse toward the children in the mothers themselves. Unlike the maternal impulse in the Western narrative tradition, which is assumed to be infinite and continually giving, continually self-sacrificial, the mother in Marchessault's novels, despite a two-hundred-year brush with Catholicism, is allowed her own interests, and is dignified by a sense of choice and limitation. In "The Angel Makers," written after *Mother of the Grass*, Marchessault portrays the mother as an illegal abortionist. After the operation, the mother and the woman she has assisted whisper together that they are not killers: "They have merely slowed the panicky course of the hypnotized toward the most negative level of life . . . they have halted succession, lunacy, family, waste, and gangrene" ("The Angel Makers," 87). Of course, Marchessault knows as we all do that this view is not currently a socially acceptable one. Her description of the angel makers is followed by a list of derogatory names, by which these women, outlaws, may be named: "The angel makers, witches, hysterical women, the bad fucks, old cows, bitches in heat, wild cats, old mares, birds of ill omen, non-virgins, whores, lesbians, unnatural mothers, loose women, crazy ladies, chattering magpies, cock-teasers, the depressed and the sluts, like those two there, have already been burnt, and they will be hanged on top of that" ("The Angel Makers," 87). It is an outburst expressing rage and fear and self-doubt all at once. Nevertheless, the narrator exclaims, emphatically, "My mother exists and that fact makes me ecstatic" ("The Angel Makers," 85). It is an assertion that most daughters of Western culture have yet to make, as affirmation and celebration.

Grandmothers, in traditional Aboriginal terms, were deemed more powerful than mothers; they were less preoccupied with the daily responsibilities of child-rearing, and their age signified seniority in wisdom and experience. In portraying the family intergenerationally, Marchessault is able to give us a sense of the traditional power of the grandmothers, without glossing over the oppression of the mothers in the modern family. A similar portrait of the grandmother, as artist and creator, can be found in Gabrielle Roy's *The Road Past Altamont*. Like Marchessault, Roy is deeply moved by the magic of landscape, earth and lake and sky, and sees the grandmother's power as connected with it. Roy's portrait does not draw on the Aboriginal tradition, but is rather steeped in French Canadian prairie Catholicism. It seems that those communities that were able to preserve a sense of the extended family against the ravages of industrialization have access to a greater range of maternal figures than those who didn't.

Marchessault's Grandmother, despite her flamboyant air, is not without her own tragic history. She buried nine babies from her first marriage, the narrator tells us, living on the trapline with her husband, and carrying their bones around with her in a little bag, before she gave birth to the narrator's father, her only living child. Her power is not the power of privilege but of experience and perseverance. Together with the narrator's family, the Grandmother and her second husband form an extended family group that makes it possible for the women to provide emotional and practical support to one another, and to offer a kind of intergenerational knowledge to the granddaughter that is sorely lacking in Western family narratives. This knowledge includes a recognition of the limits of the purely reproductive function of women and the importance of related activities, such as artistic self-expression and healing, which sustain the reproductive process and the women who are the keepers of it.

Interestingly, the narrator chooses not to replicate the oppression of motherhood by marrying or having children herself. In this sense, perhaps, Marchessault agrees with Nicole Brossard's assertion in *These Our Mothers*, that the only way to end patriarchy is for women (at this particular moment in history, at least) to stop bearing children, to get out of the family, and to create independent lives with and for one another. Brossard imagines this act of independence to be a violent one that will "kill the womb" and the mother, as well as patriarchy – images that ominously echo the fate of mothers in patriarchy. The community that replaces the family in Brossard's vision as a result is therefore primarily a lesbian/sisterly one: "It is while caressing the body of another woman over its entire living surface that she kills the mother, that the identical woman is born" (1983, 23). In Marchessault's vision, by strong contrast, the mothers stay alive and continue to play a dominant role. Brossard's text eventually takes us away from the playground where the mothers are gathered with their young children to the image of women in revolution: "I want to see in fact the form of women organizing in the trajectory of the species" (1983, 101). *Mother of the Grass* ends similarly with the narrator's artistic awakening, but her imagined universe remains profoundly maternally centred. Here is the closing passage in the novel: "And then, I told myself, perhaps one day I shall be able to create something, to testify to hope and life. Perhaps, I will even write a few lines about a grandmother, myself, Earth, the Mother of the Grass, and about a she-whale who will never mount to the surface anymore" (*Mother of the Grass*, 173). In the Aboriginal signifying system, the "(grand)mother" represents social power *as a woman*, partly because of her reproductive role and partly because she transcends it. Even though the family portrayed in this novel is caught increasingly in the patriarchal system, there is enough access to an alternative cultural vision to politicize the requisite symbolic positions, if not explode them. Song Six, on the other hand, gives a vivid and horrendous picture of the narrator working in a nineteenth-century Dickens-style garment factory. The question here is how long Aboriginal cultural groups can hold out against the pressures of industrialism; perhaps it is only a matter of time before the family tribe is irrevocably fragmented by the industrial machine, before the memory of the Grandmother is subsumed in the Western narrative of the nuclear family and its absent/ powerless mother? Marchessault's answer for now is "No! No!" The daughter refuses to get caught in the seductive net of the industrial hierarchy, refuses the place offered to her in the factory, refuses to fall in love with a male supervisor and thus reproduce the oppression of the Western nuclear family. She quits her job to become an artist and self-creator instead, drawing inspiration and strength from her now aging Grandmother.

*White Pebbles in the Dark Forests*, Marchessault's experimental third novel, published ten years after the second, provides an apocalyptic and prophetic gloss on the trilogy. Doris Cowan, reviewing this novel for *Books in Canada*, calls it a "strange book," perhaps not entirely successful, although "maybe it's just that her new, dramatic forms of expression take some getting used to" (1991, 42). Most of the novel is constructed as dialogue, between Jeanne the narrator and the community of women she lives with in the Appalachian mountains, whom she calls alternately the "red cicadas" and the "old guard." This dialogic structure is sometimes difficult to follow but allows Marchessault to explore conflicting narratives in different voices, and to discuss polemical issues without targeting individual characters. An important figure in the novel is Noria, Jeanne's lover, who arrives in a little airplane, the Spad, with her two dogs, Rimouski-Belle and Only-One-Eye. Later we find out she has rescued them from death in scientific experiments. Much of the novel is a protest against the destructive uses of modern science: the torture of animals in the name of research, and the adaptation of space technology to military ends. "What seemed, at the beginning, to be an extraordinary adventure marked by the spirit of romance," observes the narrator, referring to the beginning of aviation at the turn of the century, "was transformed, with demented speed, into a gigantic enterprise of death" (*White Pebbles in the Dark Forests*, 53). Why, asks the narrator, why does this seem to happen, so quickly, with almost everything? One reason the late twentieth-century spirit is so sick, so destructive, suggests Marchessault, is because of the extent of animal torture in our time – six billion dogs tortured to the point of death since 1945, estimates Marchessault rather extravagantly, eighteen million turtles dead with electrodes buried in their brains, six billion monkeys, rabbits, cats, mice, and calves tortured and killed, all in the name of scientific knowledge: "A billion mutilated phantoms whose shrieks of hatred for the human race haunt the Atmosphere of the Age!" (*White Pebbles in the Dark Forests,* 88).

Marchessault constructs an alternative genealogy of the universe to the current scientific one, which derives to a large extent from the Judeo-Christian one, with its mind-body split and attitude of (male) domination over nature. In Marchessault's vision, it is animals who are "the Mothers of humanity." In what she calls the Third Age, the narrator explains, "the animal reign of the Mothers began, very gently, to imagine us, the human beings, as a possible ideal" (*White Pebbles in the Dark Forests,* 29). The First and Second Ages, before that, she tells us, engendered the mineral and vegetable worlds out of the slow, beautiful process that she calls "the innovation of form." The Fourth Age, suggests Noria, "will in its turn begin to invent the future. It dreams of utopias! It delights in adoration and destruction, in cruelty and pity. In its own time, it imagines a possible ideal." In the Fifth Age, responds Jeanne, "it will be our turn to be Ancestors. Who knows what this new age will remember of us as it tells its tales and stories to its children" (*White Pebbles in the Dark Forests,* 29).

Paula Gunn Allen, describing the ancient Keres gynocratic society at Laguna Pueblo in New Mexico, explains the importance of the question, Who is your mother? in Keres discourse:

Among the Keres, "context" and "matrix" are equivalent terms, and both refer to approximately the same thing as knowing your derivation and place. Failure to know your mother, that is, your position and its attendant traditions, history, and place in the scheme of things, is failure to remember your significance, your reality, your right relationship to earth and society. It is the same as being lost – isolated, abandoned, self-estranged, and alienated from your own life. (Allen 1986, 209-10)

The figure of the Woman, Mother, Grandmother was (and is) recognized in traditional Aboriginal societies not only as powerful social figure, but as creator, as mythical source of being in the universe. In Keres culture she is referred to as Spider Woman, the being who "weaves us together in a fabric of interconnection" (Allen 1986, 11). Because she represents the life-giving spirit of the universe itself, she is deeply connected to the animal, vegetable and mineral worlds, as well as to the stars. Marchessault's genealogy of creation translates the traditional Aboriginal myth into modern "scientific" discourse in order to critique and challenge the way we behave toward the natural world in Westernized, industrialized countries. Her metaphor, "animals are the Mother of humanity," inverts both patriarchy and humanism, and challenges us to cultivate reverence toward animals and plants, since we are in fact dependent on them for our being.

And, if there is to be a Fifth Age for us to be ancestors to, Marchessault grimly reminds us (as does Laurence in *The Diviners*), there is urgent need for political action and reform, particularly in the uses of industry and technology, otherwise we will destroy the natural environment, our matrix, our Mother, altogether. Reflecting on her task as a writer, the narrator declares at the beginning of the novel: "I have just recalled that my part, a part which I have by heart but which I had forgotten in the depths of my childhood, my part, I say, is to save the world. As is yours! I am convinced that each and every one of us knows this part . . . even if we try to distract ourselves away from it. . . . Our role is to save this world, so old, beautiful, so cruel, and so tender" (*White Pebbles in the Dark Forests*, 8). According to Marchessault, it would seem we have already embarked on the Fourth Age, the age of utopias, when human actions get divided clearly into "adoration and destruction, . . . cruelty and pity." The polemical nature of current world events and philosophies tends to corroborate her view. Phyllis Webb's notion of a universal "paradigm shift" also supports this notion. The task of the reader, for Marchessault, is therefore a deeply active and political one.

The women on the Appalachian Trail attempt to nurse back to health Noria's dogs, brought to them from experimental labs across the country. Sometimes they survive. Often they must be put to death by injection. "Someday," imagines the narrator," perhaps tomorrow, the return will occur. That precious old ancestor will return who, long, long ago, imagined us in a luminous perspective, like a possible ideal" (*White Pebbles in the Dark Forests*, 89). Marchessault does not say what this ancestor will look like. Perhaps it will be one of Noria's dogs resurrected. Perhaps it will be White Buffalo Woman of Lakota myth, or Spider Grandmother, creator of the universe out of her own wrinkling.[18] Perhaps it will be the return of Marlatt's "wild mother dancing," mythical embodiment of the generative universe, made real through our recognition of her.

Marchessault is not advocating a simple return to pre-industrial, pre-technological society (even if such a thing were possible). Her novel is in many ways a celebration of technology, and particularly women's role in it. Song Three contains a list of the names of women who participated in the invention of aviation, including Maryse Bastie, Adrienne Bolland, Hélène Boucher, Jacqueline Auriol and Danielle Decure in France, Jean Batten in New Zealand, Hanna Retitsche in Germany, Jacqueline Cochran, Ruth Nichols and Amelia Earhart in the United States, May Heath, Amy Johnson, Mary Bailey in England, Moulon Embete in

Ethiopia, and Joan Bonnisteel in Canada (*White Pebbles in the Dark Forests*, 64). Noria's mother is portrayed as an adventurous, courageous aviator, whose exploits celebrate the new relationship to the sky. After her death, she appears to Noria, who is caught in her Spad in a dangerous snowstorm over the Appalachian mountains, as a spirit, and saves her life by pointing her in the only safe direction. In Marchessault's view, technology as a manifestation of the human creative spirit is a wonderful thing. What makes it destructive is the attitude of contempt for women and animals that is endemic to scientific and government institutions, and that promotes their oppression.

Part of Marchessault's interrogation of the world, which includes an honest scrutiny of her own actions, is reserved for the Fathers. Every time she asks herself about them, says the narrator, "I am up against a wall, and I hear so much weeping. And I hear the sound of all those things that have been worn away by those tears. And I hear that violent theft which was committed so long ago. The years, the centuries, the mounting mass of misery" (*White Pebbles in the Dark Forests*, 9). In this novel the Fathers are represented by the figure of Noria's father, dubbed the Lion of Bangor, who was a cancer research specialist with typical dreams of conquest and ownership toward women and toward the body. The novel ends with a moving portrait of this man, who has come to the mountains to nurse his dying daughter. Instead of trying to save her life with drugs and surgery, he very gently assists her toward death with healing colours. He tells the narrator, Jeanne, the painful story of how he came to be transformed, from a competitive, jealous male to the compassionate, gentle father he is now, through great suffering and the recognition of his own misdeeds. He also tells her the horrendous story of Noria's childhood after her mother's death in an aviation accident, including an extended stay in a camp operated by the Ku Klux Klan. After his personal awakening, the Lion of Bangor tells us, he devoted his life to finding and restoring his lost daughter, to becoming a father in practice and not just in name.

A final shocking image in the book is the Lion of Bangor's revelation that Noria had a child, who was tortured and killed in "Pavlovian" experiments, which he says were "much in vogue in the 1940s," and were practised extensively on human children as well as animals. The horror of this image overwhelms the end of the novel and emphasizes as perhaps nothing else could Marchessault's warning to us, that unless we revolutionize the way we behave in the modern world, our children are doomed.

# Silent Mothers / Noisy Daughters

Joy Kogawa's *Obasan* and Sky Lee's *Disappearing Moon Cafe*

Joy Kogawa's accomplished first novel, *Obasan* (1982), documenting the plight of Japanese Canadians during and after the Second World War, is structured, interestingly, around the absence of the mother. While the connection between Canadian/international politics and family politics is thus subtly and firmly established as narrative fact, the story of the absent mother is complicated here by its racial, cross-cultural context. The novel celebrates the cohesiveness and stability of the Japanese-Canadian family with the mother at the centre, and mourns its fragmentation through the disenfranchisement and dislocation of Japanese Canadians during the war. One of the bitter ironies in the novel is that the Japanese-Canadian community, unlike some immigrant groups (for example, Chinese, Hutterite), was working hard to assimilate to mainstream Canadian culture. Most of the narrator's family is Christian. The father, a doctor with Western medical training, plays European compositions on his violin, the mother sings English folksongs. Stephen becomes a classical pianist. Naomi is a public-school teacher in rural Alberta. "We are *Canadian*," the narrator insists over and over, as do other members of the family. There was no need to intern Japanese Canadians during the war, Kogawa asserts, because there was no opposition to "Canada" in them.

*Obasan* served as a catalyst to the Japanese redress movement in the 1980s, with people like Joy Kogawa and Roy Miki as advocates. The movement successfully defended the rights of Japanese-Canadian citizens, who were wrongfully imprisoned and robbed of their homes and land, and who were dislocated in small groups to remote geographical areas in rural Canada during the 1940s and '50s. Unlike some postmodernist fictions that cut themselves off from context entirely through extreme self-reflexivity, Kogawa's fiction is firmly rooted in historical fact, and insists on redress. Aunt Emily's passionate journal entries, documenting some of the horrors of the Japanese internment, paraphrase Muriel Kitigawa's letters to her brother Wes in the National Archives (discovered by Kogawa in the early 1980s and later edited with annotations by Roy Miki in a collection entitled *This Is My Own* [1985]). The novel, which is highly poetic and personal in style, nevertheless asserts its historicity, ending with an "Excerpt from the memorandum sent by the Cooperative Committee on Japanese Canadians to the House and the Senate of Canada, April 1946." The memorandum documents and protests the "injustice and inhumanity" of the orders-in-council for the proposed deportation of Canadians of Japanese racial origin (overlooking and condoning, however, the enforced displacement, dispossession and dispersal of Japanese Canadian citizens from B.C. to the prairie provinces and eastern Canada), thus confirming in a legal sense the extreme attitude of paranoia and racism toward Japanese Canadians that existed in Canada during the war. By linking this story of racism and political imperialism with the narrative of the absent mother, Kogawa forces us to acknowledge the connection between the forcible absence of the mother in Western social narrative and attitudes of domination toward people of other races. She also reminds us that environment and story are vitally connected to one another, that the politics of place and the politics of family, of human reproduction, are similarly and inextricably grounded in the maternal body, and that neither can achieve integrity without honouring the mother's story.

Edward Said has coined the term "Orientalism" for the West's attitude of domination toward the East, which he claims has roots in the eighteenth century and is profoundly embedded in Western social, political and philosophical practices. According to Said, "Europe gained in strength and identity by setting itself off against the Orient as a sort of surrogate and even underground self" (Said 1978, 3). He describes Orientalism as "a Western style of dominating, restructuring, and having authority over the Orient." Because of Orientalism, he says, "the Orient was not (and is not) a free subject of thought or action" (1978, 3). Said's description fits also the European attitude toward Aboriginal peoples in the Americas and elsewhere, from at least the time of Columbus. Columbus's ambition in "discovering" the Americas was to find a cheap route to India and the "Far East." Spain's subsequent plundering of North and South American Aboriginal cultures was perhaps not so different from its intentions toward the "Orient." Certainly both Kogawa and Sky Lee make a narrative link between Native and Asian North Americans. Not only do they bear physical resemblance to one another, according to Kogawa and Lee, but they share the same racist heritage in Canada and elsewhere. As many feminist scholars have asserted, the attitude of domination and subordination in Western European–based cultures is continually reinforced by and indeed grounded in the hierarchical relationships between male and female, sanctioned by marriage and the patriarchal family. "Woman" is thus linked with "oriental" and "native" in the Western European (male) imagination. The "absent mother" becomes, in *Obasan*, significantly, a metonym for silenced Japanese Canadians (and, by analogy, of all silenced cultural groups). Kogawa's title for the 1983 Japanese edition of *Obasan* was *Ushinawareta Sokoku*, "The Lost Motherland" (Redekop 1989, 16), underscoring the link between the absent mother and the loss of home for Japanese Canadians during the war.

How come, asks Kogawa over and over, German Canadians weren't sent to prison camps the way the Japanese were, if Germany and Japan were equally the enemy? Why were Japanese families broken apart and relocated to remote areas in Canada after the war, if not for reasons of genocide? "We won!" exclaims Steven, the narrator's younger brother, as the war ends, not understanding the terrible irony for Japanese Canadians in this victory, nor how closely the punishment of Nagasaki touches his own family. Rough Lock, the legendary old man of Slocan, provides a model for cross-racial dialogue here. As he says to the children playing near the river, "Never met a kid didn't like stories. Red skin, yellow skin, white skin, any skin. . . . Don't make sense, do it, all this fuss about skin?" (*Obasan*, 145). Naomi's painful confrontation of the past in the form of Aunt Emily's journal and her own struggle to find a balance between silence and speech, acceptance and political resistance, in the form of activism, is the central model for cross-racial conversation in the novel. Roy Miki describes the effect of Kogawa's project to break silence over this terrible episode in Canadian history, with Naomi as her spokesperson: "The Eurocentric and patriarchic assumptions that have determined the hierarchic structure of Canadian centralism works as long as everyone outside that circle suppresses or otherwise 'controls' the limits of their subjectivity. When those on the margins break the closures imposed on them, that Yeatsean centre – that Eurocentric form of order – 'no longer holds'" (Miki 1991, 5).

The bombing of Nagasaki, which forms the climax of this novel, as it did of the war, shows North American Orientalism escalated to proportions of unmitigated horror. In the midst of this horror, we encounter the missing mother, her face burned off, her skin charred, a survivor with a face mask, accepting and indeed insisting on her own absence and silence, to her children and to herself. What is the meaning of the silent mother in *Obasan*? In an interview with Magdalene Redekop, Kogawa discussed the mother's absence in the novel, and her reappearance at the end as a survivor of Nagasaki. "The mother's absence," she explained, "is the prime analogy for the experience of divine abandonment. God is also defaced among us. Love's presence is only understood when stripped of its potency and paradoxically its power to heal us comes when we embrace its impotence" (Redekop 1989, 17). Redekop responded by pointing out the alarming absence of the mother's subjectivity as a result: "But what about the mother? She's still voiceless. You pray to the Gentle Mother but she's still powerless. There's something there that you're exploring, that whole victim mentality and the suffering mother. It's almost as if it's the silent mother that is at the heart of the bomb. . . . And that's so painful and frightening I can't even frame a question about it" (Redekop 1989, 17).

Other critics have tried to grapple with the meaning of the mother's absence in *Obasan*, with varying results. A. Lynne Magnusson reads the novel in Lacanian terms, as a narrative depiction of the child's crisis of separation from the mother's body, which occurs at the moment of acquiring speech and entry into the symbolic order of language. According to Magnusson, Kogawa is attracted to the "consoling story of a pre-linguistic paradise" in which the child is connected to the mother, without having to speak. The longing to recover the original presence of the mother makes Kogawa ambivalent about the efficacy of language in this novel. However, as Magnusson points out, the separation from the mother does not occur at the point of acquiring language in this novel, but well after the narrator has learned to speak, and read and write. In fact, there are several separations between the narrator, Naomi, and her mother, the first a psychic separation that is caused by Old Man Gower's sexual violation of the pre-pubescent girl, an event she does not feel able to report to her mother. Her silence therefore makes her an accomplice of the old man and his abuse. This event causes a rift between Naomi and her mother, which she describes as follows: "His hands are frightening and pleasurable. In the centre of my body is a rift. / In my childhood dreams, the mountain yawns apart as the chasm spreads. My mother is on one side of the rift. I am on the other. We cannot reach each other. My legs are being sawn in half" (*Obasan*, 65). The second and permanent separation is occasioned by the mother's voyage to Japan and subsequent wounding in Nagasaki by the bomb. And, although Magnusson doesn't mention this, we might identify a third stage in the separation between Naomi and her mother, consisting of the family's conspiracy of secrecy around the mother's absence and disfigurement.

Magnusson explains the discrepancy between Kogawa's narrative and the Lacanian model as follows:

What we find . . . is a story and a counter-story, or a preferred myth of origins and unassimilated story elements that pull against it: a consoling story of a pre-linguistic paradise in tension with a supplement that threatens the consolation of the story. The violence which the Gower supplement threatens to the preferred story seems to be played out obliquely in some of Naomi's nightmares. . . . After the long-delayed "telling" of Nagasaki, after Naomi has absorbed the hurtful betrayal of the "not telling" (232), Naomi relinquishes the original myth of a pre-linguistic paradise. This revision of the past privileges speech over silence, language – with all its inadequacy – over a delusory wordless security. (Magnusson 1988, 65-66)

I would argue, rather, that Kogawa's narrative, given the particular configurations of speech and silence in relation to the mother's presence/absence in *Obasan*, does not really fit the Lacanian paradigm of language development. It is not, after all, the entry into language and speech that precipitates Naomi's separation from the mother as nurturing presence, nor is the meaning of silence in this novel primarily related to nostalgia for the undifferentiated pre-linguistic maternal body. As Magnusson rightly points out, it is (adult male) violence that pushes the young Naomi from the comfort of wordlessness, as an expression of her mother's physical and spiritual closeness – a mode of communication highly valued in the Japanese family as more intimate than speech – to a sense of alienation that feels more like the withholding of speech, of being silenced. It is adult male violence, again, multiplied a billionfold in the dropping of the atomic bomb on Nagasaki, that enforces the mother's irrevocable absence from Naomi and her family, later in the novel. The person who encourages Naomi to renounce her long silence, furthermore, even though it means contradicting her cultural upbringing and opening old wounds, is not some paternal authority figure but her Aunt Emily. We might say, given these narrative particulars, that the Lacanian model of speech development as a relinquishment of pre-linguistic maternal presence and entry into the symbolic area of the Father, with its inherent sense of distance between signifier and signified, is displaced in Kogawa's fiction by a complicated dialogue around the efficacy of speech and silence, both of which can be used as modes of communication and withholding. Aggression and violence, similarly, in Kogawa's view, are more accurately the determinant of alienation in language and in people's psyches than is the acquisition of speech *per se*. And, as many women could attest, entry into language is not condition enough to make speech possible in the context of violation and enforced maternal absence. In order for women to speak under these circumstances, Kogawa would agree, it is necessary for them to find at least one strong adult female figure who can act as surrogate or "symbolic" mother to them, to help them break silence, as Aunt Emily does here.

The ongoing debate in the narrator's mind between the worth and usefulness of silence and speech in the novel represents, also, a complex dialogue between Asian and contemporary North American cultural modes. Obasan and Aunt Emily, the two aunts, are set up as opposite models of womanly nurturing for Naomi in the absence of her mother, the one representing silence, constancy, calmness, passivity and acceptance of fate, the other representing speech, activism, anger, memory and political resistance to injustice. Each of these modes, Kogawa shows us, has its strengths and limitations. Obasan has been a warm, consoling, motherly presence for Naomi while growing up. Her "silence" gave her the strength and capacity to endure the injustices of war, and to nurture Naomi and Steven through much hardship with a measure of equanimity. Obasan's silence is not an empty silence, but a practised silence, in which we can recognize the ancient Buddhist ideal of self-discipline and acceptance of difficult circumstances, and personal restraint. On the other hand, Obasan is unable to offer much help in the way of political resistance after the war. If there is a battle to be fought, Obasan's silence is not of much use. Aunt Emily, by contrast, is angry, articulate and actively engaged in cultural politics. She is not "maternal" in the traditional sense; it is hard for us to imagine Aunt Emily consoling her niece and nephew during internment. Yet she acts as muse to Naomi in her mid-thirties; she nags at and finally inspires her niece to break silence, to investigate the history of her people's abuse in Canada, to ask questions about her mother's absence, to speak out publicly, to become politically active.

Kogawa's portrait of the mother as silent presence occurs predominantly toward the end of the novel. Young Naomi has mistakenly put the new baby chicks into the mother hen's cage, only to see the hen attack them. Naomi's mother's response is quick, non-judgemental, and reassuring to her daughter:

All the while that she acts, there is calm efficiency in her face and she does not speak. Her eyes are steady and matter of fact – the eyes of Japanese motherhood. They do not invade and betray. They are eyes that protect, shielding what is hidden most deeply in the heart of the child. She makes safe the small stirrings underfoot and in the shadows. Physically, the sensation is not in the region of the heart, but in the belly. This that is in the belly is honoured when it is allowed to be, without fanfare, without reproach, without words. What is there is there. (*Obasan*, 59)

Wild 🕴 Mother 🕴 Dancing

Later, in the house, after the chickens have been rescued, the mother and daughter have the following exchange:

"It was not good, was it," Mother says. "Yoku nakatta ne."
Three words. Good, negation of good in the past tense, agreement with statement. It is not a language that promotes hysteria. There is no blame or pity. I am not responsible. The hen is not responsible. My mother does not look at me when she says this. . . . She has waited until all is calm before we talk. I tell her everything. (*Obasan*, 60)

These passages constitute a critique of the Western tendency, deriving to a large extent from Christian practice, to impose judgement and blame on children's actions and feelings, an attitude that promotes feelings of shame and guilt in the child. Kogawa offers an alternative model of parenting, which allows the child privacy and respect, but also safety and nurturing. It is not a "pre-linguistic" relationship, but rather a relationship in which language is used with care, to convey calmness and loving acceptance of the other. By not naming or prodding at the child's emotional response, she is allowed to experience her feelings, in all their confusion and ambivalence, without having to reveal them, and therefore without shame.

Interestingly, Kogawa links the mother's use of language and silence with the steady, matter-of-fact expression of her eyes: "They do not invade and betray." There is an implicit negative comparison being made here with the Western use of language and the direct "gaze," the way both are used to confront, control and manipulate the other. Joy Asham Fedorick offers a similar critique of the Western gaze, from an Aboriginal point of view:

Dominant culture of North America dictates the use and re-
liance on eye contact as a means of determining sincerity, hon-
esty, self-confidence, etc. Yet, to the Swampy Cree, etiquette
required that you avoid direct eye contact as much as possible,
as the eyes were considered to be the "Windows of the Soul."
For one to stare into your eyes was an intrusion, and to focus
on another's was earnestly avoided. Negative stereotypes were
not assigned to his behaviour, indeed, the person who practiced
such avoidance was considered to be both respectful and humble. (Fedorick 1990, 12)

Fedorick, like Kogawa, makes a connection between the Western
use of the gaze and the tendency toward colonization, to "invade
and betray" non-Western cultures:

Yes, we're interesting to look at, analyze, and speculate upon,
take under advisement and pray for. All these things also fulfill a
further purpose: during the scrutiny of us, one procrastinates
from looking at "self." . . . We, due to the dominance of Western European culture in our lives, have had our own history
torn from us and thrown away. We are forced to live without
our history, due to the intervention of invasion. (Fedorick
1990, 10, 12)

Kogawa suggests that the Western need to dominate and control
other cultures is connected, profoundly, to the way personal
relationships are constructed, through language, through the
gaze, and through childrearing practices in the patriarchal family.
Kristeva's distinction between the semiotic and the symbolic
functions of language, and their respective associations with the
mother and father, in this sense, reflect perhaps the particular split

between body and mind, female and male, unconscious and conscious, of Western cultures, rather than the universal function of language itself. Kogawa's description of maternal language certainly suggests an alternative model, in which the semiotic and the symbolic exist carefully and respectfully in partnership with one another, rather than being structurally opposed. The language of the body is brought into the realm of words, not by alienation and subjugation, but through silence, through listening and respect.

Kogawa's description of "Japanese motherhood" is followed immediately by the narrator's description of Old Man Gower sexually abusing the young Naomi. This is the one thing, the narrator tells us, she cannot tell her mother. As Magnusson suggests, this is where the split between the daughter and mother really occurs: at the point of entry into a particular kind of language, the language of colonization, of invasion and betrayal, a language that has hidden at its centre the sexual abuse of children. The rest of the novel becomes a dialogue between the two kinds of language, the language of politeness and respect, which honours silence, the presence of the body, and the privacy of the other, and the language of direct action and speech, which tends toward invasion and betrayal. Kogawa's anguished insight is that, though the former is more affirming, the latter unfortunately becomes necessary in order to resist betrayal, once it has occurred. The narrator's moving speech to her (found) absent mother at the end of the novel addresses the limitations of the Japanese mode of language and silence in the face of racial and sexual abuse: "Gentle Mother, we were lost together in our silences. Our wordlessness was our mutual destruction" (Obasan, 243). Kogawa's novel is really a plea, in a global sense, to confront the split between East and West, between silence and speech, between contemplation and action, body and mind, female and male, mother and father, which makes sexual and cultural domination of the "other" possible. The fact that her plea is addressed first and foremost to the daughter and mother underscores the importance of this relationship in cultural terms, and suggests a revolutionary stance toward the Western attitude of devaluing and silencing the mother, in the name of the symbolic.

Susan Griffin offers a similar plea, in slightly different terms in *Woman and Nature: The Roaring Inside Her* and *Pornography and Silence: Nature's Revenge against Culture*. Griffin's argument is that Western dominant thought has tried to split the world into two hostile, opposing categories, "Culture" and "Nature," in order to control and dominate "Nature," and has reinforced this dualism by metaphorically associating women with "Nature" and building social structures to dominate them. Against this familiar traditional paradigm, Griffin offers the insight that "we see ourselves. And we are nature. We are nature seeing nature. We are nature with a concept of nature. Nature weeping. Nature speaking of nature to nature" (Griffin 1978, 226).

Marilyn Russell Rose interprets Kogawa's ongoing debate in the novel between speech and silence rhetorically, as a reply to the post-Saussurean belief in the non-referentiality of language. *Obasan*, Rose argues convincingly, "assumes that ultimately language can convey actual human experience, whatever the complexity of the relationships between language and social context. Moreover, it is overtly rhetorical in its assumption that experiencing 'real' human suffering, even indirectly, as when human experience is enacted in language, will radicalize the person who comes to know it, the reader" (Rose 1948, 215-16). Naomi's problem, according to Rose, is not with words *per se* but "with experience that is so frozen within her as the novel begins that it cannot be released into 'freeing' language – spoken language, *recorded* words, public speech" (1948, 219). Rose identifies the silence of the "victim," whether it be of sexual or other kinds of abuse, in Kogawa's terms, with the daughter's feeling of the alienation from the mother. The absence of the mother in Western narrative, that is to say, is neither accidental nor innocent. Bringing the mother, and hence also the daughter's helpless, mute self, back into the story involves an heroic act of remembering, grieving, lamenting, and ultimately of challenging the *status quo*. In Aunt Emily's words, "You have to remember. You are your history. If you cut any of it off you're an amputee. Don't deny the past. Remember everything. If you're bitter, be bitter. Cry it out! Scream! Denial is gangrene" (*Obasan*, 49-50).

What about Magdalene Redekop's "frightening" question about the silent mother at the heart of the bomb? If, as Kogawa suggests, the mother represents God, the divine presence among us, and her absence and disfigurement a sign of our lack of recognition and caring, what does that say about the explosive power contained in the heart of the atom and its destructive potential? Is that also God? Is that also the mother? Kogawa would say yes. That is after all the energy that makes life possible, the matrix, the womb of matter. It is our human responsibility, Kogawa would argue, to honour the "impotence" of God, the silence of the earth, the mother, matter, to recognize and embrace its helplessness in the face of the human will to destruction. In this sense, it is not the mother's silence that is disturbing in the novel but rather her family's, in the way that it distorts Naomi's perceptions while growing up and paralyzes the family's individual and collective responses to her disfigurement.

On the other hand, by equating the mother with God and matter metaphorically, Kogawa risks essentializing the mother as a human figure out of the realm of subjectivity and speech, though at the same time happily undercutting the traditional Christian hierarchy of spirit over matter. This may be what is most "frightening," as Redekop says, about Kogawa's vision. In a published conversation with Janice Williamson, Kogawa admits to this problem in the novel:

Debbie [Gorham] told me she thought that I had made these two female characters, Naomi's idealized mother of childhood plus the *obasan*, because I wasn't able to cope with the reality of what happened to my real mother. She had been a very bourgeois, beautiful, elegant woman with a lovely house, lovely clothes and furs, and china and furniture and music lessons. She was a musician. She had all of that, and suddenly she was out in the prairies in this dusty place and an important part of her gave up. She didn't seem to care anymore; . . . increasingly she retreated from the semblances of things that children need. It's difficult for me to talk about this. (Williamson 1993, 156-57)

Most of the time, however, Kogawa is careful to delineate the mother as human subject, particularly in her silences, which, Kogawa shows us, are themselves a kind of speech. "I am thinking that for a child there is no presence without flesh," writes Naomi near the end of the novel, after discovering her mother's fate in Aunt Emily's letters. "But perhaps it is because I am no longer a child I can know your presence though you are not here. The letters tonight are skeletons. Bones only. But the earth still stirs with dormant blooms. Love flows through the roots of the trees by our graves" (*Obasan,* 243). Through language and memory, then, and even more, through the particular sensitivity of listening to silence, the absence of the mother can be undone, even after her death. By rewriting the story, by challenging the will to dominate in the Western split psyche as reflected in its power structures, Kogawa implies, the mother (and perhaps also God) can take her place among us, as presence instead of terrifying absence.

⬤

Sky Lee's first novel, *Disappearing Moon Cafe* (1990), describes the experience of four generations of Chinese immigrants on the Canadian West Coast. Like *Obasan*, it is a novel about racism in Canada and its effect on Asian families, particularly on women. There are important structural differences between these texts, however, some of which have to do with the specific cultural context out of which each is writing. The community Lee writes about was discriminated against economically and culturally, rather than officially through the war. Unlike the Japanese families in Kogawa's novel, who are working hard at assimilating to mainstream North American life, while at the same time maintaining their own cultural and family network, the Chinese families in Lee's novel are radically separatist. They interact with "ghosts," outsiders, non-Chinese people, only when strictly necessary. They construct large economic and cultural enclaves in North American cities, "Chinatowns," which are self-sufficient to a great extent, and run by Mafia-like clan hierarchies. It strikes me as ironic that the Japanese willingness to assimilate, to participate in Western social and economic structures, should be seen as more imperialist and threatening to European-based North Americans than the Chinese attitude of separatism. On the other hand, it is easier to discriminate racially against a group that is seen as closed and irrevocably "other." Lee refers, obliquely, to the kind of street violence that Chinese youths are subject to in Vancouver as a matter of course. Her characters also refer, frequently and matter-of-factly, to the kind of trouble they anticipate from Canadian government officials regarding immigration of Chinese relatives and import/export regulations:

Under the strain of bigotry, they were outlaws. Chinamen didn't make the law of the land, so they would always live outside of it. In fact, it was a crime for them just to be here. The result was submerged, but always there: violence, with the same, sour odour of trapped bodies under duress. That could be why the whites complained that chinamen were unclean. Sinister, they said. But imagine their fresh-faced, thoughtless innocence beside the seething rage and bitterness in chinese faces! They grew uncomfortable in the presence of chinese, without even knowing why. (*Disappearing Moon Cafe*, 221)

The whole issue of racism against Chinese people flares up in the Foon Sing murder trial. Foon Sing, a Chinese house boy, is convicted of murdering his white mistress. The Chinese community, all too aware of the danger this incident puts it in, given the racial tensions of Vancouver, deals harshly and finally with the boy before he can testify in public. Lee's anger is directed in part against the European-Canadian community and its racist practices, but it is directed at least as much toward Chinese-Canadians. During the Foon Sing incident, she writes, "[the elders] were surprised to find how much alike chinamen and white people were" (*Disappearing Moon Cafe*, 223). Both groups are portrayed as harsh, unforgiving, and also terrified. In another episode she describes the beginning of the Cold War (and the resulting separation between Chinese family members on different continents) as follows: "Then, in 1949, China closed – no, slammed – its doors to the west. . . . I like to imagine Fong Mei as this cold war cartoon character I once saw in a magazine, with no other option than to stand in front of those bamboo curtains, banging her fists on them, with what she didn't realize was an empty suitcase at her side" (*Disappearing Moon Cafe*, 167).

There is less an "us and them" stance here, less a vision of unimaginable, unmitigated, and undeserved suffering among a particular people (as in Kogawa's novel), and more a sense of mutual aggression, mutual hostility between people of different races, and also between people of one race. The novel begins with Gwei Chang's experience of travelling in northern B.C. in search of his ancestors' bones, left to rot without ceremony beside the railroad in whose service they died, and his romantic encounter with Kelora, the young Indian woman with a Chinese father. His first response to her is, "But you're a wild injun," suggesting that racism is as endemic to Chinese thinking as it is to white North American thought. As we find out later in the novel, Gwei Chang abandons his son by Kelora, Ting An, after she dies, an act of betrayal that has grave consequences for his future progeny. Most of the tensions in this novel, in fact, have to do with family issues, the kinds of intergenerational wrongs perpetrated in families by parents, which then get passed on to the children. The family story, as Lee tells it, is (in the drunken words of Morgan, Ting An's son), "a story full of holes . . . no, wait! A family full of assholes, . . . assholes plugged with little secrets!" (*Disappearing Moon Cafe*, 160). The whole idea of telling a story across several generations – a rare occurrence in English literature – is itself a way of practising "reproductive consciousness," looking at the physical and emotional consequences of actions in the long term. While Kogawa's struggle in *Obasan* is to find an assertive enough voice to speak for restitution of past wrongs perpetrated by the Canadian government upon Japanese-Canadian war victims,

Lee's project is rather to uncover the family secrets, to expose the greed and contempt and insecurity that exist within the Chinese extended family, which in her view have been fed to a large degree by the narrow circumstances forced upon it by racism in Canada, but also, as the narrator increasingly recognizes, by the narrow-minded patriarchal mindset of the traditional Chinese family system.

At the heart of the novel is the secret of incest, perpetuated across several generations in the Wong family. It is a secret that Kae, the narrator, has sensed intuitively since she was born, a silent anxiety that festers in each family member, poisoning relationships until it is finally exposed. The occurrence of incest threatens the structure of the patriarchal family in a radical way. On the other hand, it may very well be fuelled by the desire to perpetuate and protect the privileges of patriarchy. The incest dynamic may even be, as some theorists have claimed, somehow endemic to the patriarchal family structure, with its premises of (male) mastery, ownership and the father's name.[19] This is why the "secret" carries so much weight in incestuous families: because the integrity of the family name and ultimately the structure itself depend upon it. As the saying goes among incest survivors, "Incest was never taboo. It's talking about it that's forbidden." In the Wong family, incest is fuelled by the desire in both mother and father, great-grandparents of the narrator, to further their social standing in the Chinese community. Both suffer a lapse in "reproductive consciousness," we might say, in the name of the symbolic, the Name of the Father/Son. Gwei Chang abandons his first-born son, Ting An, largely for racist and capitalist reasons, because his mother, Kelora, was Indian, to find a "real wife from China." Mui Lan, his Chinese wife, on the other hand, desperate for a grandson to boost her social clout, abandons her daughter-in-law, Fong Mei, and sets up a secret liaison between her son and a local waitress. The understanding is that the waitress will give up her child to Fong Mei once it is born. The waitress, however, does not conceive a child with the son, Choy Fuk, since he is impotent. This dilemma necessitates a further secret liaison between the waitress and another man, to satisfy Mui Lan. Fong Mei, the disgraced and abandoned daughter-in-law, meanwhile, becomes secretly involved in a romance with Ting An, not knowing of course that he is Gwei Chan's abandoned son. Fong Mei bears three children from this liaison, while remaining married to Choy Fuk, thus rescuing her status with her mother-in-law, but under false pretences. The waitress, on the other hand, refuses to give up her son from her second liaison. In a small, closed community surrounded by racial hostility, as Lee demonstrates, such convoluted secrets will necessarily have spin-off effects on the next generation. The children from these various marriages and liaisons end up innocently falling in love with each other and bearing children of their own, all tainted by the shadow of incest. The intergenerational tensions created in this scenario are sometimes unbearable. By the time we get to Kae, the narrator's generation, the family secret has become a very loud, unspoken presence, with "evil tentacles" (*Disappearing Moon Cafe*, 23) that reach into every family encounter.

The narrator is in the process of bearing her first child as the novel begins. Her impetus for hunting down the family secret, as writer, as "teller," thus coincides with her maternal desire, to know who her ancestors were, not just in name but in fact, in flesh and blood, to know what genetic heritage she is passing on to her newborn son. The "gaze," in this novel, is associated with anxiety of reproduction, searching for signs of incest on the face and body of each new family member. The disjunction between signifier and signified, when recognized in the context of reproduction, can be painful in the extreme. Here is the narrator's description of her mother's first look at her new baby:

> She unravels his tightly clenched fists and reads his wizened little face. She pinches his ear lobes and prods his entire skull. Peering at private parts, she is thorough, even the underarms have to be examined. Afterwards, she sits down on her chair again, looking as if she wishes with all her heart she could unzip him to continue with her search inside.
>
> "What are you looking for, Mah?" I ask, although I figure I already know.
>
> "Nothing." She suddenly stiffens in a way that is very familiar to me. (*Disappearing Moon Cafe*, 22)

Later, after unravelling the many layers of the painful, convoluted family secret, Kae and her friend Hermia are able to discuss reproductive identity in the following terms:

> Kae asks Hermia: "Is this what they call a forward kind of identity?"
>
> Hermia asks Kae: "Do you mean that individuals must gather their identity from all the generations that touch them – past and future, no matter how slightly? Do you mean that an individual is not an individual at all, but a series of individuals – some of whom come before her, some after her? Do you mean that this story isn't a story of several generations, but of one individual thinking collectively?" (*Disappearing Moon Cafe*, 189)

In other words, once the question is taken out of the patriarchal family context, with its anxious and tenuous sense of connection between genetic continuity and the family name, between the truth of the body and the truth of words, human consciousness is free to assume its own real shape, as the sum of experiences touching an individual identity. Margaret Laurence makes a similar point at the end of *The Diviners*, when Morag exchanges Christie's hunting knife for Jules's plaid pin, with its motto, "My Hope Is Constant In Thee." Clan Gunn, she recalls, did not have a crest or a coat-of-arms. But, thinks Morag, "adoption, as who should know better than [she], is possible." Reflecting on the motto further she muses, "It sounds like a voice from the past. Whose voice, though? Does it matter? It does not matter. What matters is that the voice is there, and that she has heard these words which have been given to her. And will not deny what has been given"(*The Diviners*, 352-53). Inheritance, in Laurence's view as in Lee's, is ultimately a matter of recognition of what has "been given" to make up an individual's life. Both genetic and cultural influences are possible, and, from a maternal point of view, equally valid and not necessarily the same.

*Disappearing Moon Cafe* depicts, among other things, an extended dialogue between Kae and her maternal ancestors. While Gwei Chang and his activities are highlighted as the beginning and end of the story, and while his name and identity provide the frame of this family story, it is the women whose motives and feelings are most intensely portrayed, and it is they whom Kae must come to terms with emotionally in her own quest for freedom and wholeness. The narrative framework thus threatens to invert itself. Initially, the great-grandmother, Mui Lan, and the grandmother, Fong Mei, are portrayed as greedy, grasping, scheming bitches, in contrast to the more calm and centred Gwei Chang. As the narrative proceeds, however, we are given more and more insight into these women's lives and motives. One of the

**130**

great tragedies for women in the patriarchal family is their loss of personal identity through marriage. Typically, they are forced to leave their families and friends, sometimes without ever being able to see them again, to become part of their husbands' lives. There, they are constricted by their husbands' desires and activities into a narrow social context indeed. Mui Lan's desperate wish for a grandson, at any cost, is described with a lot of anger on the part of the narrator but also, finally, with sympathy and insight. Fong Mei's infidelity, similarly, is portrayed with judgement, but she, too, is allowed to assume a place of sympathy by the end of the novel. The personal growth demonstrated by the narrator in learning to tell this story is perhaps the most powerful aspect of the novel. There is a moving scene in the chapter entitled "Feeding the Dead," in which Kae confronts the ghosts of her grandmother and great-grandmother and "has it out" with them, so to speak, once and for all. Lee is not unaware of the melodramatic potential of such a scene, and carefully builds in a parodic element:[20] "(I want a classic scenario of wailing women huddled together to 'feed the dead.' Lots of eerie mist. I want to make them weep from their own time periods and, at the same time, in harmony with each other)" (*Disappearing Moon Cafe* 188).

In spite of the "wailing" and "eerie mist," this ghostly confrontation is powerful and climactic. Fong Mei's confession, in particular, subverts the patriarchal frame of the novel in a profound and irrevocable way:

What is this Wong male lineage that had to be upheld at such a human toll? I once thought it was funny that I could take my revenge on the old bitch and her turtle son. Another man's children to inherit the precious Wong name, all their money and power. I forgot that they were my children! I forgot that I didn't need to align them with male authority, as if they would be lesser human beings without it. (*Disappearing Moon Cafe*, 189)

She goes on to imagine what her life could have been if she had claimed it for herself instead of giving it over to the Wong name:

Women, whose beauty and truth were bartered away, could only be mirrored, hand-held by husbands and men; they don't even like to think that they can claim their children to be totally their own. I was given the rare opportunity to claim them for myself, but I sold them, each and every one, for property and respectability. I tainted their innocence with fraud. (*Disappearing Moon Cafe*, 189)

This speech is not without irony, in the narrator's mind. Fong Mei's confession is immediately followed by the image of Suzie, breaking down into tears and screaming. She is the daughter of Fong Mei, who was most affected by the fraud of incest, and most victimized by it, mostly because she refused to buy into the lie, refused to play the family game. As the narrator says, "She never could be detracted from what she knew she must do" (*Disappearing Moon Cafe*, 190). Fong Mei's post-mortem manifesto to claim her children for herself, instead of for patriarchy, thus acquires a tragic ring. Not playing the game may result in less fraud, less confusion to pass on to your children, but it may also land you dead. Lee's answer to this dilemma would be for women (and mothers) to develop independent means of income, and to cultivate supportive friendships with other women, outside the family, as Kae does with Hermia.

The novel ends with the image of Gwei Chang, struggling to relax into old age but being forced to face his own misdeeds: "When he opened his dim, old man's eyes, he saw his garden was in order, everything as it should be. . . . But when he closed his eyes, he saw submerged violence" (*Disappearing Moon Cafe,* 218). Unable to undo the murder of Foon Sing, the Chinese houseboy whose legal conviction threatened the safety of the Chinese community many years before, and unable to bring about a reconciliation with his abandoned son, Ting An, whom he has employed without wages in his warehouse for many years, Gwei Chang is forced to die without recognition, a dethroned patriarch, with only the private memory of his first wife, Kelora, and her Indian simplicity, to sustain him in the hour of death.

# "Everyone has their own story to tell"

Katherine Martens in Conversation with Seven Women

In 1989, Katherine Martens recorded thirty-nine audiotaped conversations with women in the Mennonite community of Manitoba, on the subject of childbirth, which are collected in the Manitoba Provincial Archives under the title "Childbirth in the Mennonite Community." The collection also includes three conversations with men, two of them medical doctors in the community. The selection of storytellers, according to Martens, was done on a casual, word-of-mouth basis and was intended to reflect as great an age range as possible. The oldest storyteller was born in 1897, the youngest in 1966. Some of the older women told their stories in Low German, most of the younger women in English. Although Martens typically opened the conversations with a question such as, When you hear the word "childbirth," what comes to your mind? the conversations often range over a wide area of personal topics in the speaker's life. Together, these stories form a remarkable document of women's experiences in the Mennonite community, an intimate, yet public, conversation centred in the profound experience of childbirth and mothering, or in some cases of not bearing children, not becoming a mother, choosing not to have more children, or becoming an adoptive mother. (Several of the speakers refer obliquely or directly to methods of not having children, such as birth control, abstention, sterility, and abortion – potentially controversial topics in the Mennonite community, as elsewhere; however, most stay with the topics of childbearing and childrearing. Seven of these conversations were transcribed, and one of them was translated from Low German to English, by Heidi Harms, in an unpublished text entitled "Mennonite Childbirth Stories: Katherine Martens in Conversation with Seven Women," which also includes two essays by Katherine Martens about the interview process and the project as a whole.[21]

Mennonite culture in Canada, a rural-based, separatist, ethnic and religious community that traces its roots to the Anabaptist movement in Europe in the sixteenth century, has retained much of its pre-industrial, pre-Renaissance character, particularly in the farming communities of southern Manitoba, Saskatchewan, Alberta and Ontario. While Mennonite families retain a semblance of pre-Christian family structures – with extended families, elaborate gift-exchange procedures, strong matriarchal, or more precisely maternally centred, households, and active use of Low German (a non-conceptual, oral language analogous to Cree and other Indigenous languages in its lack of abstractions and its humorous, irreverent, even bawdy character) – the culture has nevertheless been marked by an extremely repressive, patriarchal Christianity that enforced strict obedience to the Church, fathers and the Bible. Artistic self-expression, individuality among community members, and particularly individual voices for women and children, were severely curtailed, mainly through repressive childrearing practices and "shunning" of nonconformist adult members, through several centuries. There has been a flowering of Mennonite art, particularly writing, in Manitoba, in the the last decade. This event coincides, interestingly, with the arrival of the electronic media in the community, a technological innovation that Mennonite culture has not been able to resist in the way that it resisted, until recently, the influence of print culture other than the Bible. With one or two exceptions, however, these artists (including myself) have had to make a dramatic break with the community in order to practise their art.[22]

Martens's "Mennonite Childbirth Stories," told privately to one woman with a tape recorder, in Mennonite women's homes, but made public through audiotaping and transcription, thus occupy a revolutionary narrative space in Canadian literature, in several important ways. The telling of these stories represents the breaking of literally centuries of public silence among Mennonite women, on a subject central to their experience of being female: the subject of childbirth. The fact that these stories were told privately, to one woman, serves to emphasize their subversive-ness as social and literary text. Most of these women would not consider themselves writers in any sense; most would not dare to speak out publicly on this or any other issue. Yet in the context of Katherine Martens's sympathetic listening ear, they are able to articulate to an amazing degree – for us all to hear – the reality of their experience in childbirth, and the way it differed from the expectations imposed on them by doctors and other male profes-sionals. In the larger framework of Canadian culture, their stories likewise break open the absence at the heart of the Western narrative tradition, to reveal a powerful body of women's experi-ences, rendered passionately and articulately in language. "To be excluded from a literature that claims to define one's identity is to experience a peculiar form of powerlessness," writes Judith Fetterley, "not simply the powerlessness which derives from not seeing one's experience articulated, clarified, and legitimized in art, but more significantly the powerlessness which results from the endless division of self against self, the consequence of the invocation [in this case] to identify as male while being reminded that to be male . . . is to be not female" (1978, xiii), and, particularily, I would add, *not maternal*. Taking its place proudly beside the other texts represented in this study, Martens's "Mennonite Childbirth Stories" thus enact and celebrate a powerful and empowering moment in the history of maternal narrative in Canada.

In her concluding essay to the project, Martens describes the interviewing process as an intensely personal exchange: "If I was distracted by worries about the tape recorder or any such thing," she writes, "it always detracted from our rapport" (1992, 207). She describes the pains she took to make sure the conversation would be interactive and dialogic rather than judgemental or objectively scientific: "The single most important necessary ingredient to make a successful tape was for me to enter into a relationship with the interviewee. . . . I concentrated on understanding each woman but not judging her. . . . I was open to whatever a woman wanted to talk about. . . . I did not intend to be coldly objective, but to be a living person who listened and responded to the story" (Martens 1992, 207). Martens's approach differs profoundly from the traditional anthropological approach to collecting oral material, which assumed that the politics of gathering oral material could somehow be divorced from the material itself and that the listener's ownership of the material unquestionably takes priority over the teller's claims. For Martens, the "politics" of the exchange is central to the narrative itself. In fact, she is careful to examine her own motives in the interviewing process, since they inevitably impinge on the conversation: "A very personal problem for me was determining why I was going to tape a particular person and whether I had ulterior motives in choosing them. Invariably something went wrong in an interview in which I had not thought through my motives, though I would not want to say there was a direct connection, it began to feel very ominous to me" (Martens 1992, 197).

The context for Martens's "Mennonite Childbirth Stories" is thus both private and public, individual and communal, and the text, insofar as it represents the lives of women coming self-consciously into narrative, into self-identified, woman-identified being, as equally "fictive" and "natural."[23] I am reminded here of Mary O'Brien's claim that the moment of childbearing, more than any other, represents the coming together of "nature" and "culture." According to O'Brien, developing "reproductive consciousness" on a global scale involves first of all paying attention to this crucial moment in which historical continuity is mediated and reproduced, through the woman's involuntary/intentional act of giving birth – in contrast to the man's alienation from nature/history from the moment of impregnation (1986). Equally important in this context is the act of community performed between speaker and listener. In Mennonite culture, where women were traditionally separated from their families at a young age in order to get married and have children, and in which absolute loyalty to their husbands and children limited extensive rapport with one another, the conversation initiated by the interviewer with one woman after another represents a profound restructuring of female relations in the community, along feminist lines.

Martens uses the image of midwife to describe her role as listener. This is a particularly rich metaphor, given the context. "I began to see the process of telling our stories as similar to that of giving birth, which is unique for every woman," reflects Martens. "I saw myself as the midwife who was there to be with her but not to dictate the structure and form her story should take." In the stories themselves, the role of midwife is contrasted, in several instances, with that of doctor. Evelyn Paetkau describes the difference as follows:

... putting the mother in full charge, and yet with all the backup and the resources there, and that it's just a very natural course of events and also that the woman follows her intuitions, you know, there's no set guidelines, and I remember her telling me that one time a mother was going through quite a long labour, I think, a difficult labour, and all of a sudden the mother said, "You know, I feel like taking a bath." And Darlene [the midwife] got the bath ready for her, and the baby was born in the bathtub, underneath the water. And it was just sort of, you follow how you feel, whereas that just never ever happens, I mean that's just the opposite of the hospital [KM: Where you follow their routine.] Yes, what the doctor wants. (Paetkau/Martens 1992, 339-40)

The trope of midwife not only highlights the personal and interactive, non-interventive nature of the interview process, but also implies a profound revisioning of the way we think about the narrative process in general. For Martens, the process is dialogic and communal. Unlike the medical doctor who puts himself at the centre of the drama of childbirth by rendering the mother passive and inert, intervening with drugs and forceps and whatever else he thinks might speed up the process, unlike the doctor of anthropology who "masters" languages and cultural events by categorizing and analyzing them for his own purposes, the interviewer here sees her role as assisting in bringing forth stories out of women's experiences, in their own voices. She is not the "expert" but a listener, a receiver. Her document is not analysis but conversation. The protest against the cultural appropriation of "voice," by Native and other non-European women writers in Canada and the United States, has been made along similar lines. Storytelling, according to this argument, whose proponents include Jeannette Armstrong, Lee Maracle, Dionne Brand, Marie (Annhart) Baker, Joy Asham Fedorick and Paula Gunn Allen, is not analagous to the scientific process of observing and recording data without regard to the feelings and wishes of the beings under scrutiny, but it is, rather, analagous to such personal and intimate exchanges as a grandmother speaking with her grandchild, or a person learning to listen to animals and trees (Allen 1986, 7).

Teresa de Lauretis has posited the term "experience" to account for the difference that women (and other marginalized people) bring to language in the Western European tradition, which in so many ways denied them subjectivity. What she means by "experience" is the ongoing process by which subjectivity is constructed semiotically and historically, through the continuous engagement of a self or subject in social reality (de Lauretis 1982, 82). This concept is useful in describing the differences Martens and her subjects bring to the interview process and the narratives they construct, which in every case run counter to the male-centred definitions imposed on them socially. Most of the women in "Mennonite Childbirth Stories" do not have access to a symbolic structure that acknowledges and validates their experiences of childbirth, even though motherhood was generally considered a requisite to full womanhood in the community. The older women, particularly, have little access to any texts that name their experiences. Pregnancy was rarely spoken about, even between sisters, or mothers and daughters. Martens refers frequently to the mode of "secrecy" surrounding childbirth in the Mennonite community, even inside the family. Some of the women interviewed have access to extensive medical information through nurses' training, personal reading, and in one case through European midwife training, though most of the literature runs counter to their subjective experience. Many of the older women entered the experience of childbirthing with little knowledge whatsoever. Maria Reimer, who raised ten children, describes her lack of information as a young bride as follows:

Before I was married, I knew very little about "being in the other time," how do you say it, "pregnant." When my younger siblings were born, we had to go to the neighbours', that was a big treat, and we didn't know for how long, but in the morning we would come home and there would be a baby! But when we were already engaged, my husband went to Chicago and worked there for a year, and during that time my eldest sister talked to me about "other circumstances," about pregnancy. And she said too, among other things, that the baby moved, in my stomach! [laughs]. And that seemed so grotesque to me, I found it so repugnant, and I thought, Oh, I am never going to get married! I would never get married! That was too terrible. And for a while I wished that Peter would never return from Chicago. But we were engaged, we had made a commitment to each other, and I knew, when he came back we would get married, but it just seemed too terrible! And so I was always between those two: I wished that he would come back; I know I would have talked about it with my other sisters, about pregnancy, but this is what I remember so very clearly. And I would have, I think, talked about it with my friends, but we knew much less than what they now know from earliest childhood on! We didn't know that. And, well, he came back in August, and on the first of November, 1924, we got married. And not even a year later, just ten and a half months later, we had a baby. And that was terrible [laughs]. (Reimer/Martens 1992, 208)

Maria Reimer goes on to describe a gruesome, terrible birth-giving, with much pain and bleeding, some of it no doubt caused by the doctor's method of assisting delivery: heavy doses of chloroform over two days ("every once in a while he would let me regain consciousness"), and tearing out the afterbirth, inch by inch, with his hand. His doctor's gown, she remembers, was completely red instead of white. She prefaces this account with an expression of narrative ambivalence: "I don't even know if I really want to say it or not." We can posit several reasons for her ambivalence: the tradition of silence and secrecy on the subject of childbirthing, fear of reliving a painful memory, inarticulate anger at the doctor's mode of assistance, and impatience with a social structure that gave so very little support to women in the difficult work of maternal labour. We can imagine silence as one of the most important social strategies available to women who have no other recourse to changing the system; by not naming the horror of medical practices around childbirth and the immense suffering inflicted on women as a result, they are "protecting" their daughters and sisters from the experience in advance, so that they will have the courage to enter marriage and undergo the same horrors themselves. They are also protecting themselves from feeling all the negative emotions attached to their experience of childbirth at the hands of a medical doctor. Maria Reimer does not criticize the doctor or his method; she probably does not have access to other methods for comparison. She reserves her criticism for her mother's presence: "My mother was there, too, but she shouldn't have been. She should not have been there. She screamed too!" (Reimer/Martens 1992, 208). She also criticizes her husband: "Sometimes I thought, Oh, if only he could understand me a bit better! He had authority over me, but if only he could understand me better! But what can you expect from a man who has never been pregnant? or has never been a woman? And a woman is built differently" (Reimer/Martens 1992, 213).

Criticism of a husband in Mennonite culture is, in my estimation, rare. The only other woman who criticizes her husband in the stories included here is Anna Fullerton, who married outside the community and is now divorced, and then she only refers to the difficult time she had with him obliquely. Maria Reimer is surprisingly forthright in this regard; however, she tempers her criticism with the following comment, which allows her to express disappointment in men while at the same time accommodating the status quo:

I sometimes think a woman should not expect too much from a man. She can love him, be submissive to him, and make him happy, but she should not expect too much; if she feels she has to pour out her heart, she has to do that with another woman, a trustworthy, devout woman, and they can understand each other better. That's how I often thought over the years. And that is what I have also experienced. (Reimer/Martens 1992, 213)

Most of the women, on the other hand, with the exception of Maria Reimer, are outspoken in their critique of the Mennonite Church and Western medical practice, and the way these institutions have mistreated women. Of course, as Katherine Martens reminds us in the Conclusion, the women speaking here represent "those who have made their peace with life and can talk about the past without overwhelming regret or too much pain" (1992, 205). Martens describes meeting with half a dozen women who changed their mind about being interviewed after their initial conversation, citing "reasons of privacy or variations on that theme. They were not inclined," adds Martens, "to disturb the past which brought feelings of sadness or depression." One elderly woman told her, "If I can't tell the whole truth I would rather not tell the story" (1992, 204). We can therefore imagine a second narrative, running alongside these stories and in counterpoint to them, in which the women either have not found accommodating strategies for their anger and pain, or in which they've accommodated so much that their voices have been suppressed altogether. This second narrative is an important one to remember when reading these stories, indeed, it is an echo that informs all Western literature, a gap in the cultural text we've inherited, the background against which the mother story must be reconstructed.

Aggie Klassen, who grew up in Russia and trained as a midwife in Germany during the First World War, offers informed criticism of North American medical practice in the area of childbirth, based on her professional and cultural experience:

You see, a midwife was judged by her good performance by having the woman bear the child without tears. Yes. It had to go a slow way, and so very few women had the problem of tearing, or they didn't cut. Except on very special occasions, and I was really surprised that that was allowed here, the fastest way, and that wasn't done the fastest way but the safest way, for the woman, for the later years, that could affect her later. (Klassen/Martens 1992, 232-33)

She does not say, "I was angry," or, "I was appalled," even though she explains with some knowledge what the dire later effects of unnecessary medical intervention could be. Martens pushes her to talk about her own experience of childbirth in Canada, asking questions such as, Did the doctor encourage her to breastfeed? Aggie Klassen replies that she couldn't breastfeed, no, probably because of the anaesthetic she was given: "My doctor, he didn't give me any answer for that, . . . he was a family doctor, . . . he should have known a little about it." This comment is followed, however, by self-criticism, another common accommodating strategy for oppressed women: "But our children were all big, so they needed more milk than maybe I had" (Klassen/Martens 1992, 235). It takes enormous strength and courage to insist on the validity of one's knowledge and experience against a powerful symbolic system designed to invalidate it, even with a sympathetic listener, even at a distance and in retrospect.

Anna Fullerton criticizes her doctor for the way he talked: "Once he said, 'You know, I might have to break your tailbone.' Oh, that did not go over very well. I think what he meant was during the delivery. . . . I found out later that that was his way, that he would talk before he thought many times. He wasn't thinking of his patients" (Fullerton/Martens 1992, 247). She remembers the kindness of one of the nurses in the hospital, by comparison: "She would come and talk with me and hold my hand and I just appreciated that so much. . . . I thought that was very normal, you know, for a woman to need another woman close by and comfort her and talk with her and hold her hand and rub her back" (Fullerton/Martens 1992, 247-48). Later, she describes the near-death ordeal of giving birth to her third child. She was haemorrhaging badly, and the doctors were busy with someone else downstairs: "After a while I could feel the life go out of me, starting at the tips of my toes, and I wasn't scared, it was a very peaceful feeling, but I had just had a baby, I had had a girl, I had two children at home, I didn't want to die! I wasn't ready to die. . . . I thought he would never get there, I thought he would never get there, I thought I would die before he got there. And nobody seemed to be in any big panic" (Fullerton/Martens 1992, 267-68). Afterward, she adds, "I was – annoyed isn't the word, I was concerned about that, how I could have gone just like that, and they had not prepared for an emergency; at least that's how I felt." The word "concerned" here is startling, given the context of a life-threatening ordeal, and suggests anger, held carefully in check, against the requirements of patriarchy. Again, it is a "warmhearted, compassionate woman" nurse on the ward who helps her through the experience by staying with her.

Despite their rhetorical stance of politeness and restraint, the women whose stories are referred to here offer substantial, detailed criticisms of medical and hospital practices. Peggy Regehr comments on the helplessness of the mother during the birthing process – being strapped onto a table, being excluded from decisionmaking, and being drugged with little choice in the matter. Peggy Regehr comments further on the enforced distance between infant and mother during the first days after birth (Regehr/Martens 1992, 278). Edith Klassen speaks critically about the doctors' advice about breastfeeding on strict four-hour schedules (Klassen/Martens 1992, 297). Aggie Klassen and Peggy Regehr complain about the lack of information about proper breast care and in some cases outright dissuasion against breastfeeding by medical professionals (Klassen/Martens 1992, 234; Regehr/Martens 1992, 279). Robyn Epp is very articulate about the confusion and disagreement about the treatment she received from hospital staff and the brutal impersonality of hospital routine

(Epp/Martens 1992, 310). Most of the women also complain about the endless, isolating labour of childrearing following the momentous occasion of childbirth.

Anna Fullerton reflects on this problem: "Later on, when I found it hard having children around me so much, and having to discipline them mostly on my own, take care of them on my own, I often thought that I should never have had children, I wasn't really a fit mother. I wasn't patient enough, I needed more room for myself. Possibly if I did it again, I would not have had children" (Fullerton/Martens 1992, 271-72). Maria Reimer, on the other hand, with characteristic humour, jokes about the endless labour of childrearing: "I have sometimes said my profession was [laughs] washing dishes and washing diapers! That was my profession! [laughs]" (Reimer/Martens 1992, 209). She describes the pleasure of seeing the "long clothesline full of swaying laundry, it was a real joy! But in the winter," she adds, more soberly, "it wasn't such a pleasure, we had to hang it outside and it was like boards, the sheets and the diapers, we would bring these stiff boards inside and then we'd put up a line inside and hang it up there and usually by morning it was dry. . . . We also boiled the laundry, so the stains would all come out, we boiled them on top of the cookstove, the white wash" (Reimer/Martens 1992, 209). For the younger women, whose families are smaller and who have more access to education and household utilities, the bigger burden is the loss of financial and social independence following their children's birth. Robyn Epp reflects, "Sometimes I wonder now, why did I have kids?! . . . because they're hard to . . . I didn't expect raising children to be quite as difficult at times as it is" (Epp/Martens 1992, 324).

Very few of the women, however, perhaps with the exception of Anna Fullerton, actually regret the experience of childbirth. Most refer to it as a transformative experience, despite the long years of unpaid labour it engenders. Maria Reimer describes the transformation as follows: "The person becomes renewed. Somehow it's an experience that I can't quite explain, but it is a renewal experience. A joyous experience. Even though it was difficult, . . . your whole body is refreshed, renewed. And even the, how do I say it, the relationship with the husband, [it's] as if it's something completely new" (Reimer/Martens 1992, 210). It is impressive and amazing to see how clear and articulate each woman is about the truth of her own experience, without much narrative support other than Martens's sympathetic listening ear and occasional prompting. The text they construct individually and together engages with the official, received language of Western culture but runs profoundly counter to it. Maria Reimer uses Biblical language to express her experience in several instances, but it is difficult for us to see their application as anything but a private interpretation. For example:

When our Peter was born, between the labour pains, I suddenly saw the heavens open. There was a circle, and I could see directly into heaven! And then the other labour pains, they were also long and difficult, I saw Jesus looking down, from the edge; from the place where I could see in, Jesus was looking down. And that was very joyous for me, it strengthened me, and gave me courage to push more. . . . And with Henry, I had those two boys, with those two the Lord wonderfully, he gave me a Bible verse, I didn't even realize that I knew it by memory: "Wir sind sein Werk geschaffen, in Christo Jesu zu guten Werken" (For we are his workmanship, created in Christ Jesus for good works). I didn't even know how I was supposed to apply it to the birth. But it just came to me, through and through: "Wir sind *sein* Werk geschaffen *in* Christo Jesu zu guten Werken." (Reimer/Martens 1992, 209-10)

Instead of making narrative connections between Maria Reimer's own experience and the larger narrative and cultural framework of the Bible, this account actually underscores her alienation from it, since we are unable to see anything in these images and verses except the extremity of her pain, and the desperate need for consolation, however irrelevant the language for it might be.

Robyn Epp uses the language of contemporary Western medical practice to describe the hospital procedures surrounding the birth of her children. This is because, as a diabetic, she has had to verse herself in medical lingo. However, when it comes to describing the emotional reality of the experience, she uses colloquial language, which contrasts sharply with the impersonality of professional medical discourse:

There was this one man, he sticks out in my mind. He did a vaginal check, and he didn't use lubricant! And he's, you know, he was really rough. My gynecologist came in, my obstetrician came in, and the nurse handed him just this disinfectant, and he said, "Where's the lubricant?! I can't do this without lubricant!" and I just thought, no wonder that other thing hurt so bad! And I was here, I felt like I was just being pressed against the wall, and it hurt so bad, because I'd only had one before, like they just never did them routinely, like my mom said she had them routinely, well I didn't, because they were doing fetal assessment, that sort of thing, they didn't do them, and this guy was so inconsiderate! (Epp/Martens 1992, 312)

Peggy Regehr uses the language of social work and feminism to describe her activities in the Mennonite community: "While I was dealing with issues of women in leadership within the Church, I was also dealing with other issues, such as spouse abuse and abortion and various other kinds of issues that affect women within the Church as much as they affect women in society" (Regehr/Martens 1992, 285). Despite her confident articulation of feminist issues in the Church, however, Peggy Regehr remembers childbirth as an "uncomfortable experience" due to complete lack of information and communication with other people on the subject. What we hear most loudly in these accounts is each woman's isolation, within a culture that professes to hold the mother in high esteem but, in fact, gives very little support for her labour. On the one hand, then, there is the received cultural text, the Bible, folk and family customs, and professional information from a variety of sources; on the other hand, there is, reluctantly and passionately, the reality of each woman's own experience, running directly counter to the dominant text. Mother stories, these women show, even in the case of devout, Mennonite, domesticated women willing to conform, to practice "obedience" to male authority and full-hearted allegiance to the "family," are revolutionary in shape.

Two stories in this collection stand apart from the rest, one for the extreme hardship depicted in it, the other for its utopian, self-directed vision. Aggie Klassen's account of growing up in Siberia under extremely harsh, prison-camp conditions, is heartrending. At one point, she describes foraging in the forest for food, using potato peelings found in a garbage dump, and sometimes grass, for soup. As Aggie Klassen describes the experience, "It wasn't enough for living and not enough for dying" (Klassen/Martens 1992, 227). Her father died of a heart attack two years after they arrived in Siberia. Her mother, Aggie Klassen tells us, died of hunger. She and her sister, aged thirteen and nineteen, decide to escape a few months later, and do so by selling their few belongings and running away through the forest. After escaping from the police on foot, they buy a ride with a trucker, who takes them through the guarded border. Their most precious belonging is their "Mother's golden ring," which they eventually sell for food and train tickets to a neighbouring city, where they find relatives to stay with. A macabre detail in this tragic mother story is that the day before they leave Siberia, the girls decide to visit the mother's grave. They quickly realize that dogs have dug up her body and eaten the flesh. All that's left is a pile of bones. Aggie Klassen's syntax breaks down in describing this memory: "Before we left, early the day before, we went to see, to my mother's grave, and here we realized that the dogs had opened the grave which was very, which wasn't as deep as we have buried our people, the bones of my mother just left, and the rest were, had the dogs, the meat, I mean the mother's body was gone" (Klassen/Martens 1992, 223). What is there to say about such an experience, even at a distance? Aggie Klassen merely continues, "So we early in the morning, we left before it was dawn and we walked about for almost three days." This is a scene in which the motif of the absent mother and the military conquest that enforces her absence, we might say, is played out with a vengeance.

The second story that stands out in this collection is Evelyn Paetkau's account of delivering a child in her home, in Altona, Manitoba, by choice, attended by her husband and a midwife. This story glows in comparison with the rest. Unlike the other women, who remember their childbirth experiences with pain and bitterness due to mistreatment by hospital staff and procedures, Evelyn Paetkau describes her home-birth experience as "very special," even though there was some anxiety in anticipating the event, including lack of support from family and friends, and even though the midwife didn't arrive until after the baby was born. Evelyn Paetkau reflects on the difference between hospital and home birth as follows: "The whole childbirth process is a very natural process, it's not like a pathology, which the doctors' approach seems to treat it as. And the other thing that we really felt with Darlene was that I was in control, you know, and that she was there to assist me, but that I was the one that was making the choices and doing the work, in a sense" (Paetkau/Martens 1992, 339). Interestingly, Evelyn Paetkau makes a connection between international politics and the possibility of home births. When her mother pressures her to have a third child, she tells us, she replied, "Off the top of my head, 'Not unless there was nuclear disarmament, world nuclear disarmament, or I could have a home birth [laughs] would I have another baby'" (Paetkau/Martens 1992, 330).

Paetkau's statement may have been made facetiously, but in fact it cuts to the heart of one of the basic metaphors of Western culture. Nancy Huston, in an article entitled "The Matrix of War: Mothers and Heroes," exposes one of the recurring epithets in Western male discourse: "How long will men make war? – As long as women have children" (1985, 153). Huston interprets this statement to mean that "men make war because women have children." She goes on to delineate how completely and consistently men have appropriated the language of childbirth and motherhood to describe the exploits of war. "How many revolutions," she asks, "have been compared to 'labor pains,' violent convulsions preceding the 'birth' of a new society?" (Huston 1989, 168). Huston attributes the metaphorical association between war and childbirth to a competitive attitude in males, who feel alienated and excluded from the childbirth process and therefore attempt to construct a narrative of male heroism based on the reversal of the reproductive cycle. Most mythical war heroes in the Western tradition, she points out, were not born of woman. Much of the cultural productivity of men in our history has

consisted in imitating and controlling and obliterating the reproductive labour of women. Huston concludes her article with the
dire warning that, unless men stop making war and women stop
having so many babies, the world will collapse under the weight of
the nuclear and demographic explosions that currently threaten
us.

Paetkau, I think, is imagining a new world scenario, in which
the energy of war is converted into "reproductive consciousness,"
so that the labour of childbearing and childrearing can be recognized as central to human life on this planet, along with the caring
use of natural resources. War, on the other hand, will become
obsolete as a means of proving male valour, once men can begin
to see themselves as supportive companions in this process, along
with midwives, instead of as competitors against and controllers of
the regenerative birth process. In this sense, her narrative of home
birth represents a moving episode in the practice of "disarmament." Brian, her husband, and the father of the three children,
participates as supportive (if somewhat anxious) companion, and
the baby is born without drugs or physical violence, and without
the kind of institutional alienation common in hospitals. Most
crucially, perhaps, the mother is allowed to remain independent
and in charge of her own labour. She is not rendered helpless or
docile or humiliated or silenced in any way during the birth
process. (Evelyn Paetkau recalls a touching moment in this regard,
shortly after the birth, when the midwife arrives: "Brian said
something about his involvement, I can't remember what it was,
and she just in a very gentle way reminded him that *I* had delivered
the baby [laughter] . . . in a very gentle sort of way, putting the
mother in full charge" [Paetkau/Martens 1992, 339]). We can
imagine this mother continuing to act in politically conscious,
independent and responsible ways after this experience. In this

way Evelyn Paetkau's narrative contrasts sharply with that of the older women represented here, whose identities were literally swallowed up by the trauma of childbirth, their lack of choice in the reproductive process, and the subsequent endless labour of childrearing resulting from far too many pregnancies and births. Like the other women interviewed in "Mennonite Childbirth Stories," Evelyn Paetkau wanted children but not too many, not enough to jeopardize her identity as an independent adult human being. Unlike the others, she seems to have found enough resources to help her practise this vision from the moment of conception onward. In this sense, her story represents a profound new beginning in the evolution of "maternal narrative" on a personal, practical scale.

# Coda

The mother stories by Canadian women writers represented in this volume show some remarkable similarities, for all their variety of cultural backgrounds and subjective differences and narrative concerns. All, for example, agree on the fact of the mother's oppression and silencing under patriarchy. All share in the political/artistic struggle to bring her back into story, and hence into public, social discourse. Each of these writers also, in her own way, affirms the metaphorical (and biological) connection between maternal narrative and concern for children and the environment. Each envisions, in more and less explicit ways, a society in which the maternal will no longer be feared and silenced and despised but, rather, protected and emulated. Each writer also imagines a time when maternity will come to be regarded as a conscious, intentional option for women rather than biological and/or patriarchally imposed necessity. These common concerns across so much cultural and personal difference indicate the emergence of a powerful women's community in Canada, which

*157*

speaks for and through the maternal, and thus, in a certain way, for us all. The commonality in these stories, their profound sense of connectedness, affiliation with the *other*, whether it be growing child or another adult or animal or tree, also points to the possibility of genuine cross-cultural, and cross-gendered, conversation in this country and elsewhere, rooted not in political systems but in earth and body consciousness. Maternal narrative in this sense offers a model of dialogue in which it is possible to say, with Hélène Cixous, "I will look for the other where s/he is without trying to bring everything back to myself" (1981, 55 n. 5). It also looks toward a future in which the world is still standing: in which enough women and men will have acquired enough reproductive consciousness to begin to reverse the destructive trends in technology and medicine and international politics that threaten us today.

Jovette Marchessault's Aboriginal, shamanic vision of the cosmic Grandmothers offers a startling challenge to readers who have been educated in the European and Oriental narrative traditions. While it takes tremendous effort for non-Aboriginal writers, like Laurence, Marlatt, Kogawa and Lee, to construct maternal narrative out of a history of maternal absence, to stay with the mother's point of view and interests instead of lapsing into the daughter's and/or father's, as our patriarchal traditions have taught us to do, Marchessault ranges easily, it seems, daringly, through the cosmos in search of maternal and grand-maternal figures, and finds them everywhere. This is so despite her grim depiction of maternity under the aegis of the Catholic Church, and the post-war poverty of inner-city Montreal, and despite Marchessault's own professed rejection of maternity as life choice. While writers like Laurence and Marlatt obliquely point toward a forgotten women's history as a model for reconstructing the mother story in our time in dialogue with the concerns of contemporary feminism, including ecofeminism and the "new science," Marchessault is able to call on the relatively recent memory of pre-colonial Aboriginal culture, as well, to assist her in revisioning the universe in feminine terms.

Marchessault's exuberant grand-maternal vision tends to corroborate Paula Gunn Allen's contention that

... the physical and cultural genocide of American Indian tribes is and was mostly about patriarchal fear of gynocracy. . . . The colonizers saw (and rightly) that as long as women held unquestioned power of such magnitude, attempts at total conquest of the continents were bound to fail; . . . the invaders have exerted every effort to remove Indian women from every position of authority . . . to ensure that no American and few American Indians would remember that gynocracy was the primary social order of Indian America prior to 1800. (Allen 1986, 3).

The same could perhaps be said about the pagan cultures of pre-colonized Europe and the patriarchal agenda that ensured that the goddess religions and stories did not survive any official histories (Read 1989, 1990; Daly 1978). In *How Hug a Stone*, Marlatt broaches the question of a more egalitarian, and woman-centred, pre-Christian European society pre-dating written records in her description of a visit to the old pre-English monuments at Avebury. While the narrative concerns of the text take Marlatt away from further speculation on this subject, and back to questions of signification and subjectivity, the possibility of a cultural memory pre-dating patriarchy lingers beyond the pages of the book, and offers a visionary model for bridging the gap between Aboriginal and non-Aboriginal thinking – like

Marchessault's sunken Atlantis – through a shared, albeit fragmented, common memory of a more maternally centred time.[24]

An important motif in the mother stories represented here is the recognition that maternal subjectivity implies also its opposite – the "not-mother." In order to be a mother, consciously, intentionally and responsibly, these writers suggest, women must be able to claim their own subjectivity, prior to and apart from the needs of others, particularly the needs of their children. Adoption and abortion are therefore, necessarily, related alternative motifs, the one signifying a gap between the act of childbirth and the act of childrearing, and the other a gap between conception and childbirth, which, according to the writers represented here (with the exception of a few of the Mennonite women interviewed in "Mennonite Childbirth Stories"), can and ought to be negotiated intentionally, by choice, by the women whose bodies are centrally in question. The fact that these particular gaps in the reproductive process have been the site of much controversy in patriarchal culture indicates how central the question of maternal subjectivity is to the construction of society. The investigation of these gaps as maternal narrative space, particularly in light of the highly problematic new reproductive technologies, and the high incidence of infertility due to industrial pollution that has occasioned the need for them, is urgently called for.[25] A further investigation of maternal narrative might look at mother stories that extend the notion of motherhood beyond the parameters of biological maternity, to adoptive and surrogate mothers, for example, Alice Munro's *Who Do You Think You Are?*, Lois Braun's *The Pumpkin Eaters*, and Marian Engels's *Lunatic Villas*. (Such a study would have to avoid, however, falling back into the old paradigm of unquestioned maternal absence.) Magdalene Redekop refers to Munro's maternal figures as clowns, mothers in disguise

(1992), which implies a whole range of displacement strategies we might examine in women's fiction around the mother's problematic absence/presence as subject. Infertility in women raises a further interesting question: How are stories of women who choose not to have children, or who can't have any, situated in relation to maternal narrative? Susan Knutson's idea of "symbolic motherhood" opens yet another rich area of investigation, in suggesting that the act of social mentoring between women is a maternal (rather than sisterly) activity, a notion that explodes the narrow parameters of maternal subjectivity in Western culture, and the whole idea of what constitutes the symbolic realm, wide apart.

A further question raised by this study, particularly by Marlatt's vision of a secret women's tradition running alongside and counter to the official history of Europe and North America, and the "Mennonite Childbirth Stories" with their strong evocation of a women's narrative tradition, however covert and unspoken, is whether indeed there is an ongoing women's cultural history we might investigate in the Western tradition as antecedents to the mother stories being written in our time. If so, my sense of the mother's absence in Western narrative, shared by such critics as Marianne Hirsch, Luce Irigaray and Adrienne Rich, asks for significant revision. I am thinking, for example, of such uncanonized texts as Margery Kempe's and Alice Thornton's autobiographies, and the tradition of quirky animal stories passed down through the generations as bedtime stories told to children, with their wily, crafty mother figures able to outwit tricksters and thieves, for example, "The Little Red Hen," "The Mother Goat and Her Seven Kids" (my own favourite as a child). Such highly popular and influential fictions as *Anne of Green Gables, Little Women* and *Uncle Tom's Cabin*, the latter of which sold more copies in the United States in its day than any other book except the Bible and was credited with halting slavery in the American South (cf. Sundquist 1986), have been present and held sway over us for generations. Were they perhaps relegated to the category of "adolescent girl's fiction" in order to disarm or deny their powerful evocation of maternal subjectivity and its revolutionary implications?[26] Midwifery, as a model for women's supportive relationships to one another, and as a powerful tradition of (secret) alternative medical practice, is another important aspect of maternal narrative that needs further investigation. Indeed, the whole question of orality as a characteristic facet of women's experience and also cultural production, particularly as it relates to the maternal, needs further exploration.

"Failed mother" narratives offer another important area of investigation in contemporary fiction – stories of those mothers who go crazy or have too many children or are otherwise disabled and/or unable to defend their daughters against violence. It would be interesting to look at how their maternal subjectivity shapes the narrative in, for example, Sandra Birdsell's *Agassiz Stories*, Margaret Laurence's *A Jest of God*, and Sylvia Fraser's *Pandora*. The new genre of incest writing might prove a particularly fruitful area of investigation in this regard, using texts such as Sylvia Fraser's *My Father's House* and Elly Danica's *Don't*. My concern, however, would be to avoid setting up these failed mothers, bearers of too much responsibility and too little social support, as post-Freudian figures of blame, thus re-inscribing the patriarchal icon of the all-powerful mother who must be killed.

Another question raised by my investigation is the iconography of the mother's body. How is the maternal body represented, brought into fiction? The mother's body, as Magdalene Redekop explains in her article, "The Pickling of the Mennonite Madonna," has often been imaged, when it is present at all, as grotesquely other, an archetypal screen, a big white "mound of maternity" on which we might project our needs and desires (Redekop 1992, 100). Examples include the grandmother in Sara Stambaugh's *I Hear the Reaper's Song* and Prin in Margaret Laurence's *The Diviners*. If we think of the mother, however, as the subject of her own story rather than the unconscious vessel of others' needs, as speaking voice situated inside the maternal body, how is her body to be portrayed? "Mennonite Childbirth Stories," along with Laurence's description of Morag giving birth to Pique in *The Diviners* and Marlatt's depiction of childbirth in *What Matters*, are perhaps as graphic and specific portraits in this regard as we have in contemporary Canadian fiction. Surely it is appropriate that the inescapably physical, intensely challenging experience of childbirth is the site at which the maternal body, as thinking, feeling, speaking subject, re-enters our imaginative consciousness in new and powerful ways.

Notes

1 Burton L. White's *The First Three Years of Life* (1975) is a recent example of well-intentioned developmental psychology, aimed at mothers (and based on Burton's observations of mothers at work), but focussed entirely on the needs of the child. Chaucer's Wife of Bath and poor, hapless Griselda are early English types embodying the metaphor of woman as unpredictable and unreliable "earthly vessel" (unreliable precisely because she does not give up her subjectivity), and shadowy, selfless caretaker and companion, respectively. Mrs. Garth in *Middlemarch* by George Eliot, Mrs. Barton in *Mary Barton* by Elizabeth Gaskell and Dolly Winthrop in *Silas Marner* by George Eliot represent fictional versions of the perfect though marginal and ultimately expendable mother. Mrs. Gerson in *The Diviners* is another such figure.

2  Wordsworth's "Ode: Intimations of Immortality," where the newly born child arrives, "trailing clouds of glory" from "imperial palaces" in the sky, to be adopted as "foster child" by Earth, the "homely Nurse," is perhaps prototypical in this regard. An interesting subversion of the absent mother convention exists in Henry Fielding's *Tom Jones*, where Miss Bridget, the biological mother of the hero, poses as adoptive mother to her own child, so she may continue to look after it and not be sent into exile! Her real identity, however, is not revealed until after her death, suggesting the impossibility of containing the energy of maternal subjectivity in this text.

3  Mary Daly gives a graphic and well-documented historical account of patriarchal violence toward women, and particularily mothers, around the globe, in *Gyn/Ecology*, a history that she describes as "the sado-ritual syndrome" (1978, 107).

4  Sophocles, *Oedipus at Colonus* (1947); William Shakespeare, *King Lear* (1986); Jane Austen, *Emma* (1986); Charles Dickens, *Little Dorrit* (1985).

5  Harriet Rosenberg claims that the severe stress factors in motherwork have been largely underestimated and misunderstood in this society. As Kathryn F. McCannell and Barbara M. Herringer explain, "It is the job design itself that creates difficulties . . . rather than some flaw in the worker's personality" (cited in McCannell and Herringer 1990).

6  Laurence doesn't explore the possibility of linking Hagar as heroine with the tradition of Islam, but she would surely have been pleased to know that her exiled, self-made rebel mother

offers a meeting point between Christianity and Islam, an observation pointed out to me by my Muslim students at the University of Winnipeg.

7 See Peter Brooks for a Freudian reading of "plot" in the Victorian novel. Brooks does not address the significance of maternal death in the novel *per se* but claims that "the high incidence of orphans in the nineteenth-century novel clearly . . . present an author with the greatest possible opportunity to create all the determinants of plot within his text" (1980, 505). Leslie Fiedler's *Love and Death in the American Novel* (1966) and Judith Fetterly's *The Resisting Reader* (1978) represent contrasting attitudes toward the typical American male narrative celebrating adventure as getting away from home.

8 See Marni Jackson, *The Mother Zone* (1992), for a popular contemporary version of this story.

9 Monica Sjöö and Barbara Mor, on the other hand, argue in *The Great Cosmic Mother* that "the fact that the human female is freed from the estrus cycle of other primates means that in woman sexuality is distinguishable from, separable from, fertility. In woman alone, among all creatures on earth, . . . biology is not destiny in the narrow reproductive sense, even if patriarchy has tried, through the dogmatic supression of [her] autonomous sexuality, to reverse this evolution" (1991, 187). In this sense, O'Brien's vision of the new historical moment in women's reproductive history is perhaps a return to an earlier condition, pre-dating patriarchy.

10  Ann Radcliffe, *The Mysteries of Udolpho* (1970); Charlotte Brontë, *Jane Eyre* (1989).

11  Margaret Laurence depicts a similar dynamic in the relationship between Rachel Cameron and her mother in *A Jest of God*. In Laurence's version, too, the daughter must come to terms with her own lack of mothering, and the dilemma of having to care for her mother without having received proper nurturing herself. Her declaration, "I am the mother now," made unconsciously under anaesthetic and again later in full consciousness to her mother, suggests that she has found enough inner strength to be able to nurture her (by now) aging mother without jeopardizing her sense of self.

12  O'Brien contrasts traditional Western male-defined concepts of history based on "alienation" from time and the reproductive process, with "female reproductive consciousness," mediated by the labour of childbirth, which she claims "negates the separation between women and genetic continuity." Women therefore stand in a relation to "*time* mediated by experience," in a way that is impossible for men, except through conceptual knowledge. O'Brien argues that both men and women need to develop a greater awareness of their relationship to the reproductive process in order to practise "reproductive consciousness" more responsibly in our time (O'Brien 1981, 151-52; see also O'Brien 1986).

13  Several (male) critics have commented negatively on this passage, suggesting that Marlatt's text lapses into "essentialism" at this point. Frank Davey, for example, reads the ending of *How Hug a Stone* as follows: "[The text] places, against the categorizing and collecting masculine, an essential feminine inside which the narrator can 'stand in [her] sandles & jeans

unveiled.' . . . Like the narrative of God the Father that suppoprts patriarchy, the counter-narrative of a primal feminine is a metaphysical one which locates the human outside of social action in an archetypal predetermination" (1989, 45). Dennis Cooley, similarly, finds in Marlatt's writing a search for "origins, beginnings, sources – always for realities that are prior to language" (1989, 72). "Everywhere," he concludes, "Marlatt seeks the essential self, unadulterated by the wrong structures of knowing. Her dream is Edenic. She dreams of return, imagines she will be restored" (Cooley 1989, 78). It seems ironic that at precisely the point where Marlatt beings to distinguish in her ongoing life narrative between the chaotic "doubleheaded mother," which has haunted the Western imagination as archetype, and the more specifically differentiated, historically situated human mother, with the image of the "wild mother dancing" beside her as a mythical embodiment of the earth's generative (birthgiving) life spirit, these critics should designate her writing "essentialist." If anything, it seems to me, Marlatt's image of the mother is finally becoming historically nameable, visible, present (in a manner quite unlike the archetype of the "doubleheaded mother") in a narrative that both recognizes the long tragic history of maternal absence in the Western tradition and the life-giving spirit of the environment.

14  Cf. Teresa de Lauretis (1989), Gayatri Spivak (1984/85), Diana Fuss (1989) and Elizabeth Grosz (1989), for an elaboration of the politics of essentialism in contemporary feminist/poststructuralist debate. Spivak argues that "the great custodians of the anti-universal" are as committed to a great narrative, the "narrative of exploitation," as are those who risk universalizing their position in order to enact a political struggle for change (Spivak 1984/85, 184).

15 R.C. Lewontin, in his recent book, *Biology as Ideology*, offers an analogous critique of modern science as a doctrine of biological determinism parading as "truth," which erroneously holds out the promise of human mastery over physical organisms through the discovery of the DNA code. Instead, Lewontin offers a picture of the universe as infinitely capable of transformation through the ongoing, continuous interaction of its inhabitants: "The relation between organism and environment is that the very physical nature of the environment as it is relevant to organisms is determined by the organisms themselves" (1991, 91).

16 Herman Melville, *Moby Dick* (1967); Mark Twain, *The Adventures of Huckleberry Finn* (1977).

17 See Eva C. Keuls's fine discussion of the splitting of the female psyche in ancient Greek discourse into opposing categories of "wife" and "harlot," distinctions that Keuls argues were maintained in Greek society with violence, and still characterize the way women are regarded socially and professionally today, for example, in the contrasting popular images of teacher and waitress (1986, ch. 8).

18 See Paula Gunn Allen, *Grandmothers of the Light* (1991), for an evocative rendering of these and other North American Aboriginal goddess stories.

19 See Lynda E. Boose (1989); Naida D. Hyde (1986); Ellen Bass and Laura Davis (1988).

20 Rita Wong, in her M.A. thesis on *Disappearing Moon Cafe,* criticizes the novel as "excessive" and "overemotional" (1992, 16). Writes Wong, "I feel embarrassed, signalling my wariness of this seemingly pure emotion and distancing myself from this pain," though she also admits that Lee's melodramatic stance allows her to rebel "against (self)censorship and realist aesthetics" (1992, 17, 31). I disagree. While Lee's emotional tone is unusual and somewhat startling, I find it both powerful and moving.

21 The Introduction was published in 1990 under the title "There is as Much Pain as Joy in Women's Description of Childbirth," in the *Mennonite Mirror* 18/6 (February):7. The Conclusion was presented at the Manitoba Writers' Guild Common Ground Conference, as part of a panel on the use of oral texts, with H.C. Wolfart, Winnipeg, October 14, 1989. "Mennonite Childbirth Stories: Katherine Martens in Conversation with Seven Women" was included as Appendix A in my Ph.D. dissertation, submitted to the University of Manitoba in December 1992, entitled "'Wild Mother Dancing': Maternal Narrative in Contemporary Writing by Women in Canada and Quebec."

22 See *Prairie Fire's* special issue, *New Mennonite Writing,* edited by Hildi Froese Tiessen and Dale Boldt (11/2 Summer 1990), for an overview and introduction to the new Mennonite art in Canada.

23 For a summary of recent theorizing on the literary nature of oral texts, see Barbara Godard (1985), "Talking about Ourselves: The Literary Productions of the Native Women in Canada."

Wild  Mother  Dancing

24 Marlatt also shares Marchessault's belief in the animate universe, as, for example, in this passage from *Our Lives*: "Black, black is what we exist in, but for the dream our bodies dance, soft, ebb & flow of breath, touching, like the sea – 'even sand,' she said, "even sand & gravel are alive'" (1980, 35).

25 See Heather Menzies (1993), "Test-Tube Mothers Speak," for a brief overview of the new reproductive technologies and the ethical questions they raise.

26 I am grateful to Judith Flynn for this observation.

References

Aeschylus. 1977. *Oresteia*. Trans. Robert Fagles. Middlesex: Penguin Books.

Alcott, Louisa May. 1946. *Little Women, or Meg, Jo, Beth, and Amy*. New York: World Publishing Co.

Allen, Paula Gunn. 1986. *The Sacred Hoop: Recovering the Feminine in American Indian Traditions*. Boston: Beacon Press.

_____. 1991. *Grandmothers of the Light: A Medicine Woman's Sourcebook*. Boston: Beacon Press.

Atwood, Margaret. 1986. *The Handmaid's Tale*. Toronto: Seal Books.

Austen, Jane. 1986. *Emma*. Middlesex: Penguin Books.

Barthes, Roland. 1975. *The Pleasure of the Text*. Trans. Richard Miller. New York: Hill and Wang.

Bass, Ellen, and Laura Davis. 1988. *The Courage to Heal: A Guide for Women Survivors of Child Sexual Abuse*. New York: Harper and Row.

Bersianik, Louky. 1988. "Agenesias of the Old World." *Trivia* 7:33-47.

Birdsell, Sandra. 1990. *Agassiz Stories*. Winnipeg: Turnstone Press.

Boose, Lynda E. 1989. "The Father's House and the Daughter in It: The Structures of Western Culture's Daughter-Father Relationship." In *Daughters and Fathers*, edited by Lynda E. Boose and Betty S. Flowers, 19-74. Baltimore and London: The Johns Hopkins University Press.

Brandt, Di. 1990. *Agnes in the sky*. Winnipeg: Turnstone Press.

_____. 1992. *mother, not mother*. Stratford: Mercury Press.

_____. 1987. *questions i asked my mother*. Winnipeg: Turnstone Press.

_____. 1992. "'Wild Mother Dancing': Maternal Narrative in Contemporary Writing by Women in Canada and Quebec." Ph.D. dissertation, University of Manitoba.

Braun, Lois. 1990. *The Pumpkin Eaters*. Winnipeg: Turnstone Press.

Brontë, Charlotte. 1984. *Jane Eyre*. Middlesex: Penguin Books.

Brooks, Peter. 1979. "Repetition, Repression, and Return: *Great Expectations* and the Study of Plot." *New Literary History* 11:503-26.

Brossard, Nicole. 1988. *The Aerial Letter*. Trans. Marlene Wildeman. Toronto: Women's Press.

_____. 1983. *These Our Mothers, or The Disintegrating Chapter*. Trans. Barbara Godard. Toronto: Coach House Quebec Translations.

Buss, Helen. 1985. *Mother and Daughter Relationships in the Manawaka Works of Margaret Laurence*. English Literary Studies, Number 34. University of Victoria.

Butler, Robert. 1963. "The Life Review: An Interpretation of Reminiscence in the Aged." *Psychiatry* 26/1:63-76. Cited on pages 38-40 in Rooke, Constance. "Hagar's Old Age: *The Stone Angel* as Vollendungsroman." In *Crossing the River: Essays in Honour of Margaret Laurence*, edited by Kristjana Gunnars, 25-42. Winnipeg: Turnstone Press.

Butling, Pauline. 1991. "Changing the Iconography of Mothers: Women Imagining Women in Western Canadian Fiction." Paper, University of Calgary.

Carr, Brenda. 1990. "Collaboration in the Feminine: Daphne Marlatt / Betsy Warland's 'Reversed Writing' in *Double Negative*" *Tessera* 9 (Fall):111-22.

Chaucer, Geoffrey. 1957. "The Canterbury Tales." *The Works of Geoffrey Chaucer*. 2nd ed. Edited by F.N. Robinson. Cambridge: Riverside Press.

Chodorow, Nancy. 1978. *The Reproduction of Mothering: Psychoanalysis and the Sociology of Gender*. Berkeley: University of California Press.

Chodorow, Nancy, and Susan Contratto. 1982. "The Fantasy of the Perfect Mother." In *Rethinking the Family: Some Feminist Questions*, edited by Barrie Thorne with Marilyn Yalom, 54-75. New York: Longman.

Christ, Carol P. 1986. *Diving Deep and Surfacing: Women Writers on Spiritual Quest*. 2nd ed. Boston: Beacon Press.

Cixous, Hélène. 1981. "Castration or Decapitation?" Trans. Annette Kuhn. *Signs* 7/1:41-55.

_____. 1991. "Sorties." In *New French Feminisms: An Anthology*, edited by Elaine Marks and Isabelle de Courtivron, 90-98. New York: Schocken Books.

Cixous, Hélène, and Catherine Clement. 1986. *The Newly Born Woman*. Trans. Betsy Wing. Minneapolis: University of Minnesota Press.

Clarke, Margaret. 1990. "Review: Margaret Laurence, *Dance on the Earth.*" *Prairie Fire* 11/3:72-73.

Coldwell, Joan. 1980. "Hagar as Meg Merrilies: The Homeless Gipsy." *Journal of Canadian Fiction* 27:92-100.

Cooley, Dennis. 1989. Recursions Excursions and Incursions: Daphne Marlatt Wrestles with the Angel Language." *Line* 13:66-79.

Cowan, Doris. 1991. "Review: *White Pebbles in the Dark Forests*, by Jovette Marchessault." *Books in Canada* (March):42.

Crow Dog, Mary, with Richard Erdoes. 1991. *Lakota Woman*. New York: Harper Perennial.

Daly, Mary. 1978. *Gyn/Ecology: The Metaethics of Radical Feminism*. Boston: Beacon Press.

Danica, Elly. 1988. *Don't: A Woman's Word*. Charlottetown: Gynergy Books.

Davey, Frank. 1989. "Words and Stones in *How Hug a Stone.*" *Line* 13:40-46.

de Lauretis, Teresa. 1982. *Alice Doesn't: Feminism, Semiotics, Cinema*. Bloomington: Indiana University Press.

———. 1989. "The Essence of the Triangle, or, Taking the Risk of Essentialism Seriously: Feminist Theory in Italy, the U.S., and Britain." *difference*1/2 (Summer):3-37.

Dickens, Charles. 1975. *Little Dorrit*. Middlesex: Penguin Books.

Dinnerstein, Dorothy. 1977. *The Mermaid and the Minotaur: Sexual Arrangements and Human Malaise*. New York: Harper Colophon Books.

Djwa, Sandra. 1972. "False Gods and the True Covenant: Thematic Continuity between Margaret Laurence and Sinclair Ross." *Journal of Canadian Fiction* 4:43-50.

DuPlessis, Rachel Blau. 1985. *Writing beyond the Ending: Narrative Strategies of Twentieth-Century Women Writers*. Bloomington: Indiana University Press.

Eisler, Riane. 1988. *The Chalice and the Blade: Our History, Our Future*. San Francisco: Harper and Row.

Engel, Marian. 1986. *Lunatic Villas*. Toronto: McClelland and Stewart.

Eliot, George. 1986. *Middlemarch: A Novel of Provincial Life*. Oxford: Clarendon.

_____. 1960. *Silas Marner: The Weaver of Raveloe*. New York and Scarborough: Signet.

Fedorick, Joy Asham. 1990. "Fencepost Sitting and How I Fell Off to One Side." *Artscraft* (Fall):9-14.

Fetterley, Judith. 1978. *The Resisting Reader: A Feminist Approach to American Fiction*. Bloomington: Indiana University Press.

Fiedler, Leslie. 1966. *Love and Death in the American Novel*. New York: Dell.

Fielding, Henry. 1950. *Tom Jones*. New York: Vintage Books.

Fraser, Sylvia. 1987. *My Father's House: A Memoir of Incest and of Healing*. Toronto: Doubleday.

_____. 1976. *Pandora*. Toronto: McClelland and Stewart.

Freud, Sigmund. 1953-1974. *The Standard Edition of the Complete Psychological Works of Sigmund Freud*. 24 vols. Ed. and trans. James Strachey. London: Hogarth.

Frye, Northrop. 1990. *The Anatomy of Criticism*. Toronto: University of Toronto Press.

_____. 1971. *The Bush Garden*. Toronto: Anansi. Cited on page 122 in Hauge, Hans. 1988. "The Novel Religion of Margaret Laurence." In *Crossing the River: Essays in Honour of Margaret Laurence*, edited by Kristjana Gunnars, 121-32. Winnipeg: Turnstone Press.

_____. 1976. *The Secular Scripture: A Study of the Structures of Romance*. Cambridge, Mass.: Harvard University Press.

Fuss, Diana. 1989. *Essentially Speaking: Feminism, Nature and Difference*. New York and London: Routledge.

Gaskell, Elizabeth. 1969. *Mary Barton*. London: Dent.

Gilbert, Sandra M., and Susan Gubar. 1979. *The Madwoman in the Attic: The Woman Writer and the Nineteenth-Century Literary Imagination*. New Haven and London: Yale University Press.

_____. 1985. *The Norton Anthology of Women's Literature: The Tradition in English*. New York and London: W.W. Norton.

Godard, Barbara. 1985. "'Body I': Daphne Marlatt's Feminist Poetics." *American Review of Canadian Studies* 15/4:481-96.

_____. 1985. "Talking about Ourselves: The Literary Productions of the Native Women in Canada." The CRIAW Papers, Number 11. Ottawa: Canadian Research Institute for the Advancement of Women.

Griffin, Susan. 1981. *Woman and Nature: The Roaring Inside Her*. New York and London: Harper Colophon Books.

_____. 1981. *Pornography and Silence: Culture's Revenge against Nature*. New York and London: Harper Colophon Books.

Grosz, Elizabeth. 1989. "Sexual Difference and the Problem of Essentialism." *Inscriptions* 5:87-101.

Hauge, Hans. 1988. "The Novel Religion of Margaret Laurence." In *Crossing the River: Essays in Honour of Margaret Laurence*, edited by Kristjana Gunnars, 121-32. Winnipeg: Turnstone Press.

H.D. 1961. *Helen in Egypt*. New York: New Directions.

————. 1973. *Trilogy*. New York: New Directions.

Hirsch, Marianne. 1989. *The Mother/Daughter Plot: Narrative, Psychoanalysis, Feminism*. Bloomington and Indianapolis: Indiana University Press.

Homans, Margaret. 1983. "'Her Very Own Howl': The Ambiguities of Representation in Recent Women's Fiction." *Signs* 9/2:186-205.

Huston, Nancy. 1985. "The Matrix of War: Mothers and Heroes." *Poetics Today* 6/1-2:153-80.

Hyde, Naida D. 1986. "Covert Incest in Women's Lives: Dynamics and Directions for Healing." *Canadian Journal of Community Mental Health* 5/2:73-82.

Irigaray, Luce. 1981. *Le corps-à-corps avec la mère*. Montreal: Les editions de la Pleine Lune. Trans. in parts by Marianne Hirsch. Cited on page 28 in Hirsch, Marianne. 1989. *The Mother-Daughter Plot: Narrative, Psychoanalysis, Feminism*. Bloomington and Indianapolis: Indiana University Press.

————. 1985. *Speculum of the Other Woman*. Trans. Gillian C. Gill. Ithaca: Cornell University Press.

————. 1985. *This Sex Which Is Not One*. Trans. Catherine Porter and Carolyn Burke. Ithaca, N.Y.: Cornell University Press.

Irvine, Lorna. 1986. *Sub/Version*. Toronto: ECW Press.

Jackson, Marni. 1992. *The Mother Zone: Love, Sex and Laundry in the Modern Family*. Toronto: Macfarlane, Walter and Ross.

Jacobus, Mary. 1988. "'The Third Stroke': Reading Woolf with Freud." In *Grafts: Feminist Cultural Criticism*, edited by Susan Sheridan, 83-110. London and New York: Verso.

Jung, Carl, et al. 1968. *Man and His Symbols*. New York: Dell Publishing.

_____. 1967. *Symbols of Transformation: An Analysis of the Prelude to a Case of Schizophrenia*. Princeton, N.J.: Princeton University Press.

Kahane, Claire. 1985. "The Gothic Mirror." In *The (M)other Tongue: Essays in Feminist Psychoanalytic Interpretation*, edited by Shirley Nelson Garner, Claire Kahane and Madelon Sprengnether, 334-51. Ithaca and London: Cornell University Press.

Kamboureli, Smaro. 1991-92. "'Seeking Shape. Seeking Meaning': An Interview [with Phyllis Webb]." *West Coast Line* 6 (Winter):21-41.

Kempe, Margery. 1985. *The Book of Margery Kempe*. Excerpted in *The Norton Anthology of Women's Literature: The Tradition in English*, edited by Sandra M. Gilbert and Susan Gubar, 22-27. New York and London: W.W. Norton.

Kertzer, Jon. M. 1974. "The Stone Angel: Time and Responsibility." *Dalhousie Review* 54:499-509.

Knutson, Susan. 1991. "Imagine Her Surprise . . ." *Tessera* 10 (Summer):5-12.

Kogawa, Joy. 1982. *Obasan*. Boston: David R. Godine.

Kristeva, Julia. 1980. *Desire in Language: A Semiotic Approach to Literature and Art*. Ed. Leon S. Roudiez. Trans. Thomas Gora, Alice Jardine, and Leon S. Roudiez. New York: Columbia University Press.

_____. 1986. "Semiotics: A Critical Science and/or a Critique of Science." In *The Kristeva Reader*, edited by Toril Moi, 74-88. New York: Columbia University Press.

_____. "Stabat Mater." 1985. *Poetics Today* 6/1-2:133-52.

_____. 1981. "Women's Time." Trans. Alice Jardine and Harry Blake, *Signs* 7/1:13-35.

Lacan, Jacques. 1977. *Ecrits: A Selection*. Trans. Alan Sheridan. New York: Norton.

Laurence, Margaret. 1974. *The Diviners*. Toronto: McClelland and Stewart.

_____. 1968. *The Stone Angel*. Toronto and Montreal: McClelland and Stewart.

Leach, Edmund. 1973. "Complementary Filiation and Bilateral Kinship." In *The Character of Kinship*, edited by Jack Goody, 53-58. Cambridge: Cambridge University Press. Cited on page 22 in Boose, Lynda E. 1989. "The Father's House and the Daughter in It: The Structures of Western Culture's Daughter-Father Relationship." In *Daughters and Fathers*, edited by Lynda E. Boose and Betty S. Flowers, 19-74. Baltimore and London: The Johns Hopkins University Press.

Lee, Sky. 1990. *Disappearing Moon Cafe*. Vancouver: Douglas and McIntyre.

Lessing, Doris. 1969. *The Four Gated City*. London: MacGibbon and Kee.

Leviton, Richard. 1992. "Through the Shaman's Doorway: Dreaming the Universe with Fred Alan Wolf." *Yoga Journal* 105 (July/August):48-55, 102.

Lewontin, R.C. 1991. *Biology as Ideology: The Doctrine of DNA*. Toronto: Anansi.

Maeser, Angelika. 1980. "Finding the Mother: The Individuation of Laurence's Heroines." *Journal of Canadian Fiction* 27:151-66.

Magnusson, A. Lynne. 1988. "Language and Longing in Joy Kogawa's Obasan." *Canadian Literature* 116:58-66.

Marchessault, Jovette. 1985. "A Lesbian Chronical from Medieval Quebec." *Lesbian Triptych*. Trans. Yvonne Klein. Toronto: Women's Press.

_____. 1988. *Like a Child of the Earth*. Trans. Yvonne Klein. Vancouver: Talonbooks.

_____. 1989. *Mother of the Grass*. Trans. Yvonne Klein. Vancouver: Talonbooks.

_____. 1985. "The Angel Makers." *Lesbian Triptych*. Trans. Yvonne Klein. Toronto: Women's Press.

_____. 1990. *White Pebbles in the Dark Forests*. Trans. Yvonne Klein. Vancouver: Talonbooks.

Marlatt, Daphne. 1988. *Ana Historic: A Novel*. Toronto: Coach House Press.

_____. 1983. *How Hug a Stone*. Winnipeg: Turnstone Press.

_____. 1979. "In the Month of Hungry Ghosts." *Capilano Review* 16/17:45-95.

_____. 1980. *Our Lives*. Lantzville, B.C.: Oolichan Books.

_____. 1990. "Self-Representation and Fictionanalysis." *Tessera* 8 (Spring):13-17.

_____. 1984. *Touch to My Tongue*. Edmonton: Longspoon Press.

_____. 1980. *What Matters: Writing 1968-70*. Toronto: Coach House Press.

_____. 1986. "writing in order to be." In *SP/ELLES: Poetry by Canadian Women,* edited by Judith Fitzgerald, 66-67. Windsor: Black Moss Press.

_____. 1977. *Zócalo*. Toronto: Coach House Press.

Martens, Katherine. 1989. "Childbirth in the Mennonite Community: An Oral History Project." Audiotaped interviews. Provincial Archives of Manitoba.

_____. 1992. "Mennonite Childbirth Stories: Katherine Martens in Conversation with Seven Women." Translated and transcribed by Heidi Harms. Appendix A in Brandt, Di. 1992. "'Wild Mother Dancing': Maternal Narrative in Contemporary Writing by Women in Canada and Quebec." Ph.D. dissertation, University of Manitoba.

_____. 1990. "There is as Much Pain as Joy in Women's Description of Childbirth." *Mennonite Mirror* 18/6 (February):7.

McCance, Dawne. 1990. "Julia Kristeva and the Ethics of Exile." *Tessera* 8 (Spring):23-39.

McCannell, Kathryn F., and Barbara M. Herringer. 1990. "Changing Terms of Endearment: Women and Families." In *Living the Changes,* edited by Joan Turner, 57-66. Winnipeg: University of Manitoba Press.

Meisner, Lucille. 1990. "The Look: Women and Body Image." In *Living the Changes*, edited by Joan Turner, 136-44. Winnipeg: University of Manitoba Press.

Melville, Herman. 1967. *Moby Dick*. New York and London: W.W. Norton.

Menzies, Heather. 1993. "Test-Tube Mothers Speak." *Canadian Forum* (July/August):5-11.

Miki, Roy. 1991. "The Subject of Subjectivity." Paper presented at the Manitoba Writers' Guild Conference, Winnipeg, Manitoba, October 1991.

_____, ed. 1985. *This Is My Own: Letters to Wes and Other Writing on Japanese-Canadians, 1941-1948, by Muriel Kitagawa*. Vancouver: Talonbooks.

Miller, Alice. 1981. *The Drama of the Gifted Child*. Trans. Ruth Ward. New York: Basic Books.

_____. 1990. *The Untouched Key: Tracing Childhood Trauma in Creativity and Destructiveness.* Trans. Hildegarde and Hunter Hannum. New York, London, Toronto: Doubleday Books.

_____. 1984. *Thou Shalt Not Be Aware: Society's Betrayal of the Child.* Trans. Hildegard and Hunter Hannum. New York: Farrar Strauss.

Montgomery, L.M. 1976. *Anne of Green Gables.* Toronto: McClelland and Stewart–Bantam Ltd.

Munro, Alice. 1971. *Lives of Girls and Women.* New York: Signet.

_____. 1979. *Who Do You Think You Are?* Toronto: Macmillan.

Neumann, Erich. 1956. *The Great Mother: An Analysis of the Archetype.* Trans. Ralph Manheim. Princeton, N.J.: Princeton University Press.

O'Brien, Mary. 1986. *The Politics of Reproduction.* London and New York: Routledge and Kegan Paul.

_____. 1981. "Feminist Theory and Dialectical Logic." *Signs* 7/1:144-57.

Ong, Walter. 1982. *Orality and Literacy: The Technologizing of the Word.* Middlesex: Penguin Books.

Orenstein, Gloria Feman. 1987. "Jovette Marchessault: The Ecstatic Vision-Quest of the New Feminist Shaman." In *Gynocritics: Feminist Approaches to Canadian and Quebec Women's Writing*, edited by Barbara Godard, 179-98. Toronto: ECW Press.

Pollack, Sharon. 1981. *Doc.* Toronto: Playwrights Canada.

Radcliffe, Ann. 1970. *The Mysteries of Udolpho.* New York: Oxford University Press.

Read, Donna. 1989. *Goddess Remembered.* 54 min. video, National Film Board of Canada.

_____. 1990. *The Burning Times.* 56 min. video, National Film Board of Canada.

Redekop, Magdalene. 1992. *Mothers and Other Clowns: The Stories of Alice Munro.* London and New York: Routledge.

_____. 1989. "The Literary Politics of the Victim." *Canadian Forum* 68/83 (November):14-17.

_____. 1992. "The Pickling of the Mennonite Madonna." In *Acts of Concealment: Mennonites Writing in Canada,* edited by Hildi Froese Tiessen and Peter Hinchcliffe, 100-28. Waterloo: University of Waterloo Press.

Rich, Adrienne. 1990. "Compulsory Heterosexuality and Lesbian Existence." In *Women's Voices: Visions and Perspectives,* edited by Pat C. Hoy II, Esther H. Schor and Robert DiYanni, 290-312. New York: McGraw Hill.

_____. 1979. *Of Lies, Secrets and Silence: Selected Prose, 1976-1978.* New York: Norton.

_____. 1986. *Of Woman Born: Motherhood as Experience and Institution.* Tenth anniversary edition. New York and London: W.W. Norton.

_____. 1985. "When We Dead Awaken: Writing as Re-Vision." In *The Norton Anthology of Women's Literature: The Tradition in English*, edited by Sandra M. Gilbert and Susan Gubar, 2,044-56. New York and London: W.W. Norton.

Rooke, Constance. 1988. "Hagar's Old Age: *The Stone Angel* as Vollendungsroman." In *Crossing the River: Essays in Honour of Margaret Laurence*, edited by Kristjana Gunnars, 25-42. Winnipeg: Turnstone Press.

Rose, Hillary. 1983. "Hand, Brain, and Heart: A Feminist Epistemology for the Natural Sciences." *Signs* 9 (Autumn):73-90. Cited on page 191 in Eisler, Riane. 1988. *The Chalice and the Blade: Our History, Our Future.* San Francisco: Harper and Row, 191.

Rose, Marilyn Russell. 1988. "Politics into Art: Kogawa's *Obasan* and the Rhetoric of Fiction." *Mosaic* 21/3:215-26.

Rosenberg, Harriet. 1988. "Motherwork, Stress and Depression." In *Family Bonds and Gender Divisions: Readings in the Sociology of the Family*, edited by Bonnie Fox, 379-99. Toronto: Canadian Scholars Press. Cited on page 64 in McCannell, Kathryn F., and Barbara M. Herringer. 1990. "Changing Terms of Endearment: Women and Families." In *Living the Changes*, edited by Joan Turner, 57-66. Winnipeg: University of Manitoba Press, 64.

Roy, Gabrielle. 1984. *The Road Past Altamont*. Trans. Joyce Marshall. Toronto: McClelland and Stewart.

Ruddick, Sara. 1980. "Maternal Thinking." *Feminist Studies* 6/2:342-67.

Rush, Florence. 1981. *The Best Kept Secret: Sexual Abuse of Children*. New York: McGraw Hill.

Said, Edward W. 1978. *Orientalism*. London and Henley: Routledge and Kegan Paul.

Scheier, Libby. 1990. *SKY*. Toronto: Mercury Press.

Scott, Gail. 1989. *Spaces like Stairs*. Toronto: Women's Press.

Scott, Walter. 1925. *Guy Mannering, or, The Astrologer.* New York: Macmillan Co.

Shakespeare, William. 1986. *King Lear*. Middlesex: Penguin Books.

Sjöö, Monica, and Barbara Mor. 1991. *The Great Cosmic Mother: Rediscovering the Religion of the Earth*. San Francisco: Harper.

Smith, Paul. 1988. *Discerning the Subject*. Minneapolis: University of Minnesota Press.

Sophocles. 1947. *Oedipus at Colonus*. Trans. E.F. Watling. Middlesex: Penguin Books.

Spivak, Gayatri. 1984-85. "Criticism, Feminism, and the Institution." *Thesis Eleven* 10/11:184.

Stambaugh, Sara. 1984. *I Hear the Reaper's Song*. Intercourse, Pennsylvania: Good Books.

Stowe, Harriet Beecher. 1966. *Uncle Tom's Cabin*. New York: New American Library.

Sundquist, Eric J. 1986. "Introduction." In *New Essays on "Uncle Tom's Cabin,"* edited by Eric J. Sundquist, 1-44. Cambridge: Cambridge University Press.

Swayze, Walter E. 1988. "Knowing through Writing: The Pilgrimage of Margaret Laurence." In *Crossing the River: Essays in Honour of Margaret Laurence*, edited by Kristiana Gunnars, 3-24. Winnipeg: Turnstone Press.

*The Shorter Oxford English Dictionary*. 1973. 3rd ed. rev. Edited by C.T. Onions. Oxford: Clarendon Press.

Thornton, Alice. 1875. *The Autobiography of Mrs. Alice Thornton, of East Newton, Co. York*. Ed. C. Jackson.

Tiessen, Hildi Froese, and Dale Boldt, eds. 1990. *New Mennonite Writing. Prairie Fire* special issue 11/2 (Summer).

Tostevin, Lola Lemire. 1989. "Daphne Marlatt: Writing in the Space that Is Her Mother's Face." *Line* 13:32-39.

Twain, Mark. 1977. *The Adventures of Huckleberry Finn*. New York: W.W. Norton.

van Herk, Aritha. 1987. *No Fixed Address: An Amorous Journey*. Toronto: Seal Books.

Warland, Betsy. 1984. *Open is Broken*. Edmonton: Longspoon Press.

White, Burton L. 1975. *The First Three Years of Life*. Englewood Cliffs, N.J.: Prentice-Hall.

Williams, David. 1988. "Jacob and the Demon: Hagar as Storyteller in *The Stone Angel*." In *Crossing the River: Essays in Honour of Margaret Laurence*, edited by Kristiana Gunnars, 81-98. Winnipeg: Turnstone Press.

Williamson, Janice. 1991. "It Gives Me a Great Deal of Pleasure to Say Yes: Writing/Reading Lesbian in Daphne Marlatt's *Touch to My Tongue*." In *Beyond Tish*, edited by Douglas Barbour, 171-91. Vancouver and Edmonton: NeWest Press/Line.

_____. 1980. *Sounding Differences: Conversations with Seventeen Canadian Women Writers*. Toronto: Toronto University Press.

Wolf, Fred Alan. 1991. *The Eagle's Quest: A Physicist's Search for Truth in the Heart of the Shamanic World*. New York: Summit Books.

_____. 1981. *Taking the Quantum Leap: The New Physics for Nonscientists*. New York: Harper Books.

Wong, Rita. 1992. "Pressuring the Surface: Approaches to Melodrama in Sky Lee's *Disappearing Moon Cafe*." M.A. thesis, University of Alberta.

Woolf, Virginia. 1985. *To the Lighthouse*. London: Triad Grafton.

Wordsworth, William. 1965. "Ode: Intimations of Immortality from Recollections of Early Childhood." In *Selected Poems and Lyrics by Williams Wordsworth*, edited by Jack Stillinger, 186-91. Boston: Houghton-Mifflin Co.